Oriental Basics

cooking

home

your

to

magic

add

to

need

you

All

D1509499

Cornelia Schinharl   Sebastian Dickhaut

BARNES
& NOBLE
NEW YORK

Sebastian Dickhaut...

lives in Munich where he writes books and
magazines articles on food and drink.
He is a regular contributor to several food
magazines. Sebastian helped develop the
concept of the Basics book series and wrote
the text for Oriental Basics. Currently, his
favorite dish is Cornelia's saffron onions.

Cornelia Schinharl writes cookbooks and is
instinctively attracted to good things in any
guise, especially edible ones. She wrote the
recipes for this book, magicking up some
Oriental pleasures of the palate that anyone
can cook.

© 2004 by GRÄFE UND UNZER VERLAG
GmbH, Munich

This 2006 edition published by
Barnes & Noble, Inc. by arrangement with
GRÄFE UND UNZER VERLAG GmbH, Munich

Picture credits:

**engels zahm + partner, agentur für
kommunikation, Thomas Jankovic**
Title page fig, all illustrations

Barbara Bonisolli: all recipes; product shots
pp8/9 (except pickled lemon); still lives p24
(hookah, chessboard, cushion); insets pp41,
42, 43, 45, 53, 55, 64, 68, 78, 91 (lentils),
101, 116, 117, 119, 139, 149 (pistachios), 151,
154; Back Cover (orange lime granita, p148)

Axel Walter: all people/action shots with the
Basics models; inset pp3, 8 (pickled lemon),
25 (lamp), 34, 47, 48, 56, 61, 71, 77, 80, 81,
83 (matches), 89, 91 (dates), 99, 100, 103,
105, 115, 118, 120, 126, 136, 140, 141, 147,
149 (cutting an orange), 152; Back Cover
(model, teapot)

Bettina Gousset: pp2, 4/5, 6, 7, 12, 14, 15,
16, 18, 19, 20, 22, 23, 24 (except cushion,
hookah, chessboard), 25 (except lamp), 28,
29, 31, 72, 83 (tomatoes), 92, 109, 110, 128,
142; inside back flap (bank notes)

**iPUBLISH GmbH, GANSKE INTERACTIVE
PUBLISHING:** map inside front flap

Production:

bookwise Medienproduktion GmbH,
Munich

This edition translated and typeset by
Silva Editions Ltd, Purley

Translators: Sylvia Goulding, Rafael Pauley
American editor: Adèle Linderholm
Project manager: Sylvia Goulding

ISBN-13: 978-0-7607-8442-6
ISBN-10: 0-7607-8442-6

Printed and bound in China

1 3 5 7 9 10 8 6 4 2

Oriental
Basics
Contents

Front flap: The Orient at a glance
Back flap: Oriental almanac

Know How

Where are you from? From the Orient.

It has been quite some time since we discovered Italian food and made pizza and pasta our favorite dishes. Our weakness for Asian cooking, thanks to curries and the wok, has become an everyday affair. Yet somehow, something is still missing... What is there between the Mediterranean and Asia? That's right, the Orient! Of course that is our next trend. Perhaps not a trend, more of a really good friend, and not for the first time either. The Orient was actually Europe's first culinary love. Long before the potato came from Latin America and the pizza from Italy, Europeans were being spoiled by oranges from China, cinnamon from Ceylon, and figs, coffee, and pistachio nuts from Oriental gardens. It introduced the wonderful world of spices and of bartering, it brought color and wisdom, taught the art of genuine hospitality, and last but not least, gave us the doner kebab. And there is much more! My friends, here we come.

A European asks someone he meets: "What do you do?" But in the Orient the question that is asked is: "Where are you from?" So let us be Oriental and enigmatic too: apricot, tarragon, cinnamon, and sugar—which of these words comes from Arabic? The answer is all four. As do coffee and confectionary, marzipan and nutmeg, syrup and sherbet. That is how close the Orient is.

The spice rack—without Constantinople's traders would be almost empty. The knife block—without the Oriental blacksmiths it would be bare. The cookbook—without Arab numerals, would be guess work. Let us go to a Turkish grocery store, where the best tomatoes and the freshest lamb is found. And to one of our favorite fast-food eateries, the kebab house. The Orient is not only near, it has already arrived.

And it's red-hot trendy. Arabic appetizers, known as "mezze" (more about these from page 34) are challenging sushi and tapas; foodies are rediscovering the Turkish cuisine, trendsetters are dreaming of North Africa, couscous, and hookahs. And we are feasting on magical tales and recipes from the Middle East. We cooked with Said and asked him how to make the ras-el-hanout mixture, we baked with Hassan and discovered the secret of flatbread, we drank mocha with Pedram and listened to tales of life in Iran. We realized that the Orient connects: the Mediterranean with Asia, generous hosts with curious guests.

And so, to avoid going straight on to the kebabs, there is only one solution: Let us sit down together to share a meal, and ask the question, "where are you from?" The answer often lies closer than you might think.

17
Basics that everyone knows

Sesame seeds

Your link: Sprinkled on bread tops.
Even more than poppy seeds, sesame seeds are a must in the Oriental kitchen—they're used as a paste in tahini, as seeds sprinkled onto flatbread, mixed with nuts and spices to make a *dukkah*, and sweetened in honey bars or halva. The shelled, pale seeds are most frequently used; they are at their most aromatic when freshly toasted. Unshelled brownish seeds and slightly oily black seeds are also available and used for sprinkling over bread or other dishes.
Magical with: honey + cumin + pancakes + yogurt.

Eggplant

Your link: A Mediterranean staple.
Originally from India, this vegetable is common in Italian and Greek cooking. In the Orient it is a star, also known as "poor man's caviar." You can do almost anything with an eggplant in the kitchen—it takes on the flavor of spices, adds substance to vegetarian dishes, and flavor to famous recipes such as Babaganoush and Imam Bayildi. If you salt it, it won't take up too much oil when you fry it—although that would be a pity if you're using a quality olive oil.
Magical with: garlic + olive oil + feta cheese + ground meat + cumin.

Lemons

Your link: Basic Cooking.
Without lemons, there are no Basics Books, no fragrant groves, and no gardens in the Orient. Their juice adds acidity to *tabouleh* and aromatizes grilled food—pomegranates, sour grapes, or sumac were used before people had lemons. It was Oriental cuisine that discovered how lemons can be candied with sugar to make a sweet confection, and that they can be pickled with salt to make a spicing ingredient.
Magical with: herbs (lemon juice) + spices (lemon zest) + casseroles (pickled).

Yogurt

Your link: That carton in the fridge.
In the west it is the dieter's friend or it may be the food of choice for urban joggers whose sparkling fridges are filled with probiotic foods. In the Orient, however, "yog'urt" still has an ancient ring about it, from the days when the Asian Turkish tribes introduced it from Constantinople to the Oriental lands. Lumpiness and acidity are countered by a higher fat content. Made from sheep, goat, or even camel milk, it is ideal for dips, marinades, and *labane*—sour cream cheese with olive oil.
Magical with: cucumber + mint + honey + rosewater.

Parsley

Your link: Herb garden must-have.
We know, of course, that the green curls can be much more than a tired garnish on a sandwich platter or on top of potatoes. But we may not be exactly ready to come home from the market with huge bunches of flat-leaf parsley, to toss whole handfuls into tabouleh, onto pita breads, or into a ground meat mix. Parsley is the Oriental herb *par excellence*, which can be combined with almost anything on these two pages.
Magical with: mint + coriander + garlic + sumac + lemon + raisins.

Raisins

Your link: Cakes and muesli.
In this book, we use the term to stand for all dried grapes, from the small, firm currant to the soft golden raisin. But the indisputable star among these dried fruits is the large seedless sultana, especially those from Turkey. They add a juicy sweetness and spiciness without even a trace of sulfur. Raisins are a great snack food. They're used in many sweet desserts, but they're also a very popular ingredient in savory dishes.
Magical with: pine nuts + aniseed + rice + spinach + carrots + lamb + quinces.

Garlic

Your link: Bread and spaghetti sauce.
While the classic garlic dishes such as *aïoli*, *tzatziki*, *spaghetti aglio e olio* hail from the northern banks of the Mediterranean, garlic is an essential on the southern shores too. In fact, Ottoman and especially Persian cuisine treated garlic as a useful but less important ingredient, while today farmers and Bedouins still rate it highly as an aromatic boost for their food and the body—taste it in the Turkish *cacik*, a refreshing cucumber salad, and in Morocco's *harissa*.
Magical with: scrambled eggs + couscous + walnuts + parsley & mint (for fresh breath).

Apricots

Your link: Pies and jam.
Is there anything quite as sad as apricots drowned in syrup and then confined in a can? There is—it's apricots that have been harvested too soon. They taste bland and wooly, and it is hard to imagine the sweet, scented, and sensual aroma they can add to an Oriental salad, casserole, or dessert. If that's all there is, then use dried apricots instead—either sulfured, brightly colored, and tasting sweetish-sour or the unsulfured, dark, and sweet ones.
Magical with: parsley + yogurt + chili + goat cheese + lamb + almonds.

Pistachios

Your link: Ice cream and salted nibbles.
Only a few decades ago, the mysteriously green ice-cream scoop promised us an adventure in a cone. And today there's still a hint of decadence about sitting on the porch while nibbling these nuts and drinking a cold beer. Pistachios are fully ripe when the shell is wide open (or "smiling"), they're fresh when the skin underneath is red, and they're very expensive when shelled and green. When dry-roasted they are delicious but much less so if cooked.
Magical with: lemon salt + olives + marzipan + honey.

Honey

Your link: Breakfast buns and pancakes.
In the land of milk and honey, it is part of the first meal of the day, served on bread. But that's not the end of it: This fascinating product of blossom and bees has been used here as a sweetener since ancient times. Long before the discovery of cane sugar, it had asserted its place as an aromatic symbol for wealth and fertility, used in desserts, pastries, salads, dips, as well as savory casseroles.
Magical with: mint + thyme + cream cheese + carrots + almonds + cinnamon.

Oil

Your link: All those bottles in the supermarket.
The oil used for cooking in Oriental cuisine has undergone a few changes. Once, oil was made from sesame seeds and used for both oil lamps and stewpots. Then the olive made its appearance, and olive oil became the Orient's favorite cooking oil. Today, however, most oil is made from sunflowers or, in Morocco, from the argan fruit (more about that on the next page).
Magical with: figs, cream cheese, parsley (olive oil) + pasta, rice, couscous (argan oil).

Cheese

Your link: Greek and Turkish deli shelves.
An Oriental breakfast also includes milk, but it's sheep or goat milk, and it's enjoyed in the form of cream cheese, a product that develops almost naturally in the heat and one that keeps much better than milk. It becomes firmer when preserved in brine, like the Turkish feta cheese, and has a particularly firm consistency when it is blanched in boiling water like the Lebanese hallumi.
Magical with: mint + lemon pepper + walnut + olives + melon + honey.

Kebabs

Your link: Barbecue staple.
The home of the shish kebab skewer, threaded with meat and vegetable cubes, is somewhere between the Caucasus and the Bosporus, where Asia and Europe, the Balkans, and the Orient meet. Like yogurt, it was the Turkish people who brought it along with them when they came from Asia and arrived in Byzantium (today's Istanbul). Today the shish kebab (a meat skewer) is popular all the way to Morocco, grilled over charcoal, preferably using lamb.
Magical with: lamb & feta cheese kebab + bread & tomato kebab + fig & olive kebab.

17

basics that everyone knows

Cinnamon

Your link: Toast and apple pie.
You could almost think of it as a sweet spice, it's so intimately linked with sugar. Originally, the roll of dried bark from the laurel tree came from Ceylon (Sri Lanka) but cinnamon has become "the" spice of the Orient, where it is combined with salty, sour, and spicy as well as sweet foods. It was the merchants of the Orient who discovered the value of cinnamon for the entire world. The sticks can be enjoyed freshly ground with a pestle and mortar, or whole.
Magical with: raspberry vinegar + olive oil + tomato soup + carrots + burgers.

Sardines

Your link: Those distinctive cans.
Tuna, salmon, crab, and the trendy anchovy have almost ousted the humble old sardine. Yet young sardines, slowly cooked in olive oil and later enjoyed straight from the can, whole and with their tender bones, are really a great delicacy. They come mainly from North Africa, where the raw "herrings of the south," weighing no more than 3 1/2 ounces, are often grilled.
Magical with: dill + omelette + tomato + olives + raisins + lemon + orange.

Lentils

Your link: Soup and the vegetarian's friend.
In Oriental soups, lentils are sometimes whole, sometimes puréed. But they're also included in dips, salads, casseroles, purées, and much more besides. They're a super-food: a side dish as well as a substitute for rice or pasta; they're an alternative for meat and can be made into sauces. They set off spices, keep forever, and, compared with other legumes, they're really quick to cook—especially the typically Oriental red lentils.
Magical with: cilantro + mint + garlic + olive oil + orange juice + cinnamon.

Mint

Your link: Tea, chocolate, and toothpaste.
It's refreshing and cleansing. That we know as gum chewers and toothbrushers. And people of the Orient like to chew on fresh mint leaves after a meal, or drink lots of sweet mint tea before. If it tastes of chewing gum, then it's peppermint. Some aromatic varieties, such as the Oriental nana mint, have a better flavor: It forms a delicious contrast to spicy foods and stews. Dried mint is also used in the Orient.
Magical with: olives + feta cheese + white cabbage + chili + lentils + hazelnuts + melon.

1001 Spices & Flavors

Take a deep sniff of cinnamon—and you'll be ready to set off on a journey of discovery through time and space in the vast universe of the spice rack.

"What we have standing on our spice rack all looks pretty tame to me: pepper, of course, nutmeg for soups. Some curry powder for Indian dishes, cinnamon without which apple pie is boring. OK, so that's not so great. Excuse me? Did we know that some of the greatest fortunes and the harshest poverties, the most amazing discoveries, and the most fiercely fought battles were all caused by these few spices? That at one point a few pounds of mace was worth as much as an entire cow, and that the European explorers only set off to discover America because of curry, and that people once believed that cinnamon came from the nests of fantastic giant birds in Arabia? Magical and hard to believe. What? We are going to take a deep sniff of cinnamon, close our eyes, and then we'll see? All right then. Mmmm..."

Follow the spice route

Vast caravan routes once extended from Mesopotamia, Babylon, or Persia to Asia in order to collect the most exotic of spices.

At first it was all about cloaking your own palace in the scents of cinnamon from Ceylon (now Sri Lanka) and nutmeg from what is today Indonesia, in addition to the flavors of dill, fennel, cardamom, caraway, saffron, and thyme from your own garden. Quickly the famous spice routes of the Oriental traders reached the Mediterranean Sea. From there they took their spicy wares by boat to Europe, where they were sold at high prices. The Arabs were the first to invest heavily in this trade (holding the monopoly, they concealed their sources with scary tales, such as that of the giant birds); they were followed by the Turks.

To cut a long story short: From the 11th century onward the crusaders and the pilgrims came from Europe to the east and discovered the wonderful world of spices.

Back home spices also became popular but expensive. This was exploited by the Venetians, since the only trade route linking Europe with the Orient emanated from their harbor. Finally the Ottomans took control of the spice routes, forcing the Portuguese to sail around Africa directly to the spice sources in India and Indonesia. Christopher Columbus tried to reach these sources for Spain via the west, but only managed to discover America. He nevertheless brought back fiery chilies. And as soon as these arrived in the Orient, they were added to the range of commonly used spices, a small consolation for the lucrative trade in spices that had been lost.

What spices?

The peoples of the Orient have managed to keep hold of one thing—the art of marrying a number of seemingly opposing aromas in such a way that even the simplest of meals becomes a banquet. A spoilt Frenchman would hardly be impressed by a simple lamb kebab or a vegetable tajine. Yet as soon as ras-el-hanout, with its countless spices, a handful of cilantro, or a few drops of rosewater are added, the dish becomes sophisticated. The Moroccan cuisine, which was further refined during the French occupation, has today become "the" fashionable Oriental food. This example also shows that flavors in the Orient do not only come from spices, but also from fresh herbs, without which tabouleh and mezze would be flavorless. And that's not all there is to be found in the Oriental world of flavors: Flowers and their essences are as much a part of it as fruits, whose zest, flesh, juice, and sometimes even seeds give a meal that extra something. It is typically Oriental that a salty recipe is sweetened, soured, or sharpened by fruit.

Back to the spices: If you use them whole, and dry-roast, then grind them just before using them, their flavor is at its most intense. How is it then, that every picture we see of a bazaar shows bright cones of ground spices? First, because a mound of radiant yellow turmeric powder is more visually pleasing than its raw state, a knobbly brown root. Second, because these roots have often only just been dried in the sun, on the roof of some neighboring house, and third, because the powder is used up as quickly as we use flour, and thus has no time to lose its magical flavor. Those of us who do not consume such large quantities of spices would do better to grind what is needed shortly before use, and to store any ground spices such as ginger and turmeric in a cool, dark, and dry place until needed. So please get rid of the little transparent glass jars.

Oriental Basics:

Spices

What you should have:

Chili, cardamom (which stays fresh much longer in the pod), cilantro seeds, cumin seeds, nutmeg, cloves, plus at least one Oriental spice blend such as *baharat, ras-el-hanout,* or *za'atar* (page 113) as well as *pul biber* (a Turkish blend of hot dry spices made up of chili and paprika, used for sprinkling or seasoning), saffron threads, sumac (slightly sour-tasting red staghorn berries, usually coarsely ground), and cinnamon sticks.

What you could have:

Fenugreek seeds (yellow, slightly bitter seeds found in curries and Oriental spice blends), ginger (the dried and ground powder), fennel seeds, turmeric (a bright yellow spice, which gives curries their golden color), mace, black cumin (an aromatic and slightly bitter variety of cumin).

Aromas

Argan oil (rare, precious, and expensive oil from Morocco's argan trees, tasting like sesame and hazelnut, and like truffle oil, it adds lots of flavor with each drop). **Flower water** (from roses, orange trees, lavender, and others; used mainly to flavor sweet foods and drinks). **Pomegranate** (seeds and juice for salads and ragouts, for a Persian flavor). **Harissa** (fiery North African spice paste with lots of chili, see page 95 for recipe). **Pickled lemons** (lemons marinated in salt, also North African, see recipe page 131). **Smen** (clarified, salted, and sometimes spiced butter, which ripens or "fouls" with warmth; gives a North African aroma and scent).

Herbs

Dill, cilantro (very important in North Africa), bayleaf, mint (especially the nana variety), parsley, and thyme are the Basics; basil (only in Iran), oregano, rosemary, and sage are also used occasionally.

Where are you from...
...rosewater?

My family comes from the area around Isfahan, so it is said. Some 3,000 years ago the Persians discovered how to distil our beguiling charm into bottles (despite the fact that some claim it was the Arabs a thousand years later). At any rate, they did so for the sake of my big sister, rose oil. Today she is still produced by extracting the essential oils from the rose leaves with steam, which condenses back into a liquid. The excellent oil finally separates from this liquid. It is then exported from Turkey and Morocco to the perfume makers of France. What remains is little me, and I am much loved across the Orient. I am married with honey, cardamom, or sun-ripened fruits. I also have a little sister, known by the name of orange-flower water. She really adores hot foods.

& Breads Cereals

No matter where or when you arrive in the Orient, there will always be a piece of fresh bread awaiting you. The cereals also appear to have been here for all time.

It is true that bread in some form seems to be a part of most cultures. Yet nowhere is bread so vitally necessary at table as in the Orient. Here, it is the foundation of everything that emerges from the kitchen, from morning to night. Its aroma magically wafts through every traditional Oriental house even as you just begin to open your tired eyes. The secret to this magic: the woman of the house. She often prepares the dough the day before, and then has the daughter carry the loaves to the village baker the next morning at dawn. Some families still bake their own bread, while others, mostly those in towns, get their bread, as we do, from the bakery. The difference is that they do not go there every couple of days, they go for each meal. This is because two rules apply to bread in the Oriental routine: It must be fresh (which it does not stay for very long) and it must be finished by night. This is a matter of respect for God's most important gift and which is actually a cult-object in all the Oriental religions.

Godly unleavened bread

Even without prayer, a good Oriental bread can bring you to your knees. For the people of the Orient, there are hundreds of types, both leavened and unleavened. For the European baker, only one is of real importance—bread made from yeast dough. And yet, as those who like Oriental food will know, unleavened bread can vary quite a bit. On the one hand are the perfectly round loaves with soft crusts (the result of the plastic bag in which they are wrapped), and a toast-like center. This is supposedly of Turkish ancestry, although we suspect that a few generations of Euro-bakers lie between. On the other hand is unleavened bread, as we love it: thin and

crispy, with golden ridges that are polished like rare wood and which make it easier to break. Inside it smells divinely and has large pores which offer space for dips and salads. To make it this way, the raw dough is placed in an extremely hot oven, directly onto a stone. It rises and browns so quickly that it creates a sort of pocket rather than many small pores. This makes it perfect for Oriental meals. For bread is not spread or turned into sandwiches there; it is a pocket for a fine filling, a plate for tasty garnishes, and above all it is cutlery: Experts tear off a piece, grip it with the crust facing out between thumb, index, and middle fingers, and dunk humus, fork up tabouleh, or spoon lentil soup.

The nomads in the desert had no need for an oven to bake their bread. They laid their thin oatmeal cakes made from ground grains and water onto the red-hot stones around their camp fires or placed them on a metal plate which they laid over the embers. This made a very thin crispy bread, similar to today's bread, made from layers of yufka or filo pastry. When it was discovered that the dough turned sour and light when standing for a long time, sour dough was born (apparently in Egypt), replaced later by the Romans with their yeast dough. From India came the clay oven or "tandoor," which became the *tandir* in Turkey. The bread stuck to its hot sides while baking, just as it does in India.

Oriental Basics:

From couscous to rice

The people of the Orient worship bread-because it comes straight from God and because it hails from their own soil. Wheat and its rustic sister, barley, both originated in Arabia where nomadic Bedouins and Berbers harvested and dried the grain, and produced a number of half-finished products, from bulgur to couscous. However the Oriental creative spirit did not really take off until the nomads settled, began to farm the land, and started growing cereals in a systematic way. They soon worked out which type was best for producing which product. Here again, it is said that the Egyptians were at the head of the race by a nose length.

While African millet has only ever played a secondary role in Oriental cuisine, rice from Asia is very important. Once again it was the Persians who delighted the Orient with a product from India. Their rice dishes full of nuts, fruits, spices, and vegetables are, even now, representative of the best of Persian cooking. These were taken by the Arabs and Ottomans to Egypt and beyond. Pilafs like tchello, prepared with long-grain rice, should remain as loose and as fine as Indian basmati. Short-grain rice is used for desserts such as rice puddings or as a filling as in stuffed vine leaves.

Bread & Pastry

Pide and pita (Turkish), Khubz (Arabic), eish shami (Egyptian), Kesrah (Moroccan): Round or oval bread made from yeast dough and often covered with seeds or spices; airy inside, small loaves are also backed "hollow" so they can be filled.

Semit and Simit (Turkish): Rings of yeast dough covered with sesame seeds.

Matzo: Unleavened Jewish bread which is baked flat and crispy. Its origin lies with the exodus from Egypt to the Promised Land, during which the Israelites were unable to let the bread rise.

Fatta: Arab dish where stale bread soaked in broth is the base ingredient.

Fattoush: Arab bread salad (similar to tabouleh) made with tomatoes, herbs, and lemons, much loved in Lebanon and Syria.

Filo or Phyllo (Arabic), Yufka (Turkish): Thin pastry used in multiple layers for bread and baking, similar to strudel pastry. Sold in Greek and Turkish grocery stores as well as most well-stocked supermarkets, refrigerated or frozen.

Where are you from...
...couscous?

I come from the Mahgreb, as the Arabic people call "the land of the setting sun," seen from their own lands in the east. I come from North Africa, the Arabic Occident. They also named the nomads who lived there the "Berbers," although the latter preferred to call themselves the "free men." These free men needed provisions, in order to avoid becoming dependent on

Cereals

Bulgar: Wheat grain which is parboiled, dried, and ground into coarse granules varying in color from light to dark brown. It is then soaked and used for salads (tabouleh) or beef burgers (kibbeh).

Semolina: Finely to coarsely ground, but not powdered, wheat that is used for baking and desserts (semolina pudding, halva). Kishk or tarhana is a thick porridge made from semolina and yogurt, which is then dried, rubbed, and used to thicken soups—a sort of Oriental roux.

farming or bakers. And this is why they invented me, couscous. To make me they traditionally mixed the semolina and the flour of durum wheat with water, then slowly rubbed the mixture between their hands to make round grains, and finally dried me. I may turn out to be coarse, medium, or fine-grained. In the last guise, I am particularly popular. Traditionally I am steamed in a couscousière, where a colander-like vessel is placed over a pot of ragout or another liquid. This method is labor-intensive and time-consuming. And that is why I have a speedy brother, the presteamed instant couscous for extra fast cooking. But take my word for it, I am the more fragrant one.

& Vegetables Legumes

First, fresh produce and then some dried goods—everything that is to be found in a typical Turkish grocery store.

Arms full of vegetables

If there is one thing you will notice at a Turkish grocery store, it is that people leave it with boxes in their hands and plastic bags full of fresh colorful vegetables on their arms. The produce has no time at all to turn gray and wrinkled here. Vegetables are important in Oriental cuisine, and good vegetables especially so. And this is what we may find at a Turkish store, at least when compared to the vegetable section of most of our supermarkets. And when we are after a particularly authentic Oriental flavor—that is, sunny and intense—then it's worth respecting the seasons (bell peppers in winter just taste of nothing). We should also seriously consider buying from the local farmer or farmers' market, or from an organic or health food store.

The colorful world of legumes

The local Turkish grocery store is a veritable jungle full of secrets and things one has never before seen. The one thing you will never see is vegetables on display indoors rather than on the street outside. Cars, pollution? Well, the produce won't be there for long anyway. How enticing is the vibrant tide of shiny purple eggplants and richly green spinach, sprinkled with bell peppers in traffic light colors and brightly red tomatoes! A sight to warm the heart, just like a well-stoked oven warms a disk of freshly baked aromatic flatbread. There is so much mouthwatering produce here, the customers will all appear as if by magic, drawn in by the colorful display.

There is one area where our Turkish (or Moroccan, Iranian, or Lebanese) store remains unbeaten: the dried vegetables section. Red, yellow, orange, green, black, white, striped, or spotted, in every shape and form, from all angles, eye-catching objects that were long regarded as bland and therefore boring—yes, we are talking about legumes. In cooking, they are categorized as something between cereals and vegetables. But like meat, they provide the body with valuable proteins, iron, and vitamin B. That's why for thousands of years dried lentils, beans, peas, and garbanzos have been one of the most important foodstuff Basics for African, Arab, and other Oriental cuisines. As with grains, the nomads were able to harvest and dry them for their long journeys, usually when still in their pods. This enabled them to prepare dishes which were like meat, vegetables, sauce, and tummy filler all rolled into one. Ultimately this produced a soup like the Arab Ramadan soup with garbanzos or a porridge made of beans such as the Foul, which in Egypt has become breakfast, a snack, and the national dish.

An added bonus is the fact that legumes can absorb some of the most wonderful flavors. They give substance to almost all the Oriental spices, enlivened with handfuls of freshly chopped herbs. Salty, spicy, sour, even fruity or sweet—anything is possible for a meal made with legumes. A stick of cinnamon, a bay leaf, chili, garlic, lemon zest, or a few cardamom pods can completely transform their taste. They can, however, be ruined by salt and acids when these are added at the outset and simmered with the legumes: These will stop the legumes from softening as they are cooked.

The golden rule for cooking legumes is this: The thicker and older they are, the more time they will take to cook. This is true right from the soaking stage. Soaking involves covering the dried legumes with around twice their volume of water, and leaving them to soak anywhere from overnight (most beans) to an entire day (garbanzos). Those cooks who don't have that much time for soaking, or those who have forgotten to get the legumes into water early enough, should first cook the beans or gabanzos in unsalted water for 3 minutes, this reduces the soaking time by at least half. The legumes do however lose a little in taste and texture.

Cooking instructions are harder to generalize. Lentils take less time (red lentils almost half an hour, green lentils just under an hour) than beans, although that depends on the type, and garbanzos normally take longest. What is more, how "fresh" the legumes are is also more important than you might think. In the Orient you buy them in the bazaar, and they are from the same year's harvest, yet by the time they reach us, some time may have passed. Products which are near their "best before" dates or have even gone past them, often take much longer than usual to cook, which does little to improve them.
So when buying, try not to over-buy to stockpile, and, after opening, store lentils beans, peas, and gabanzos in an airtight container in a cool and dark place.

Oriental Basics:

Legumes

Lentils: Red and yellow (both hulled and split) are the most common, they do not need to be soaked, and cook quickly (under 30 minutes); brown, green, or plate lentils are available in sizes ranging from caviar to dimes and can be soaked, which helps them become softer and cook (at most 1 hour) uniformly.

Beans: Fava beans (also known as broad beans) were, up until the discovery of America's colorful bean varieties, the only bean in Africa and Europe. In summer you can buy them fresh, and they can then be cooked in 15–30 minutes depending on their age, having first been freed of their pods and hulls. Black-eyed beans also come from America (light beans with a dark spot like an eye) as do borlotti beans (sprinkled brown and white, or with red when fresh)—these, like dried fava beans, take at least 1 1/2 hours to cook.

Vegetables

Traditional ingredients (because they originally came from the Orient, the Mediterranean, or India): eggplant, artichokes, green beans, cucumbers, carrots, and other root vegetables, white cabbage, chard, okra (fleshy pods from a type of hibiscus plant that resemble zucchini or beans), spinach, all kinds of onions.

Only in use for a few hundred years (because they originally came from America): pumpkin, sweet corn, bell peppers (especially pointed ones), tomatoes, zucchini.

Where are you from...
...garbanzo?

Originally I came to the Orient from India, where the Egyptians cultivated me and Oriental traders exported me as far as Spain. My pods are dried and threshed in order to get to me. Then I am soaked and cooked to make a stew or humus, roasted to make delicious snacks, or ground for flour. My Spanish name? It is thought to have entered Spanish from the Basque word "garbantzu," formed from garau "seed" and antzu "dry."
At any rate, inshallah.

& Nuts Fruits

Turkish honey or Turkish fruit? Pines or date palms? Pistachio or pomegranate? Where to start?

We discussed in the last chapter how the display of fresh artichokes and eggplant outside the shop invites us to go inside where we add some garbanzos to our basket. When we get home, we just have to eat Oriental. Since this always means starting with some snacks and finishing with fresh fruit, we will cover them in the same sequence here, but in reverse order from the vegetables: first the seeds, then the fruit—first dried, then fresh.

Something to snack on

It is custom in the Orient to snack on a few pistachio nuts, a handful of roasted sunflower seeds, or even a couple of salted green almonds with a cup of tea. Not only will this get the stomach juices flowing, but it also provides a good dose of protein and fat—not a bad thing given that the Oriental cuisine is almost vegetarian. This is also one of the reasons why nuts, seeds, and kernels are present in Oriental sweet dishes like baklava and spicy sauces such as tarator, a sort of white pesto made with—depending on the region—either nuts or seeds.

All these nuts and seeds benefit from being toasted in a dry skillet or in the oven, which makes the brown and somewhat bitter hazelnut and almond skins easier to remove. For almonds this works even better if you first boil the nuts for 4–5 minutes in hot water, then refresh them under cold water before rubbing off the skins. Another 10–15 minutes in the oven at 200 °F to dry, and they are done. Even if it means a little more work, it is worth buying whole nuts for Oriental cooking, and then to chop or grind them yourself. Ready-ground hazelnuts and almonds are fine for cookies and cakes, but in a dip or a salad, their lack of flavor soon becomes apparent.

Freshness is also important: Packed in bags or cans, with their skins or peeled, most nuts and seeds will last for up to one year or sometimes even longer. They are, however, only really good for the first six months, and the slightly greasier pine nuts only for the first 1–2 months. Once opened, nuts and seeds can change flavor within days, especially if they have been chopped or ground. In this case the best solution is to store them in an airtight container in the refrigerator. And: Don't buy too much, and use up what you have.

Finish with the proud fruit

If you want to eat authentically Oriental food, you must not economize on the fruit. Mountains of oranges, fistfuls of figs, or an enormous watermelon are not only signs of wealth in the desert; they also make preparing a dessert easier. A morsel of ripe fruit is a great way to end an Oriental meal, perhaps refined with a few drops of rosewater, a dash of lemon juice, or some honey. Often fruit makes its first appearance earlier on in the meal. For in Oriental cooking, fruit—i.e. sweet, sour, or juicy flavors—is regularly combined with savory foods—i.e. spicy or salty flavors. In Persian dishes, for example, pomegranate seeds are liberally sprinkled over the rice and in Turkey feta cheese is served with figs. And just as these two fruits are symbols of the Persian and Ottoman cuisines, the date is a symbol for Arab cuisine, and in fact for the entire Oriental cuisine. More about that on the far right.

One of the greatest culinary discoveries from the Orient is sun-dried fruits, which once fortified the nomads in the farthest reaches of the desert. Figs, apricots, or grapes (fresh or dried) are to be found in many Oriental cooking pots and tajines.

Oriental Basics:

Nuts & Seeds

Hazelnuts: Popular especially in Turkey and Egypt, hazelnuts are an essential ingredient in sweet foods like halva and Turkish honey, and in savory foods such as sauces and dukkah, a nut and spice mixture (recipe page 37).

Walnuts: Cultivated by the Persians where they are often combined with pomegranates, they are also used in Turkey, for example in dips.

Almonds: Also came to the Orient via Persia, along with marzipan and almond milk. Go well with chicken, fish, and rice. A rare delicacy: green, unripe almonds which are eaten salted with their skin left on.

Pine nuts: These are often sprinkled on top of dishes, often in combination with raisins or pomegranate seeds. They add an aromatic twist to many meat and vegetable dishes.

Sunflower seeds: Generally peeled, roasted, and salted, as a snack or used in salads and appetizers.

More about **Pistachios** and **Sesame seeds** on page 10.

In the U.S.A. the dried varieties are most commonly found in muesli or snacks. In the end it all comes together—fruits and nuts, East and West.

Fruits

Pomegranates: Originating from Persia, these are acidic (forebear of lemon and vinegar) or sweet (what we generally find in the west). If they are heavy, which is rare in the west, they will be very juicy and can be pressed in a lemon squeezer—watch out for stains!). Their seeds refine any dish; the syrup—bright red grenadine—adds flavor; as molasses they give strength.

Melons: In the Orient watermelons are commonplace, and a cross between a honeydew melon and a cantaloupe melon is also popular. They are preferred on their own or with only a few flavorings such as rosewater.

Quinces: These are the basis of the first jams, made with honey, which became "marmalada" in Portugal and marmalade here. Can also be made into syrup or paste, and can be used in stews.

Grapes: Originally from the region between Tiflis and Tehran, they were made into wine—as mentioned in the Bible—until this was forbidden in most of the area by Islam. Today they are eaten fresh, dried as raisins, and their vine leaves are pickled.

Citrus fruits: These came from the Far East to the Middle East. Limes are often dried and cooked, salted lemons (recipe page 131) spice up many Oriental dishes in the Maghreb area, and orange blossoms are distilled to an aromatic water. Interesting: Oranges were initially known as Chinese apples in many languages, but the Arabic name "naranji," from the Sanskrit "narang," became "orange" and prevailed.

More about **Apricots** and **Raisins** on page 10, about **Figs** on the flap.

Where are you from...
...date?

I am a real desert child, born in the shadow of the palm trees of the oasis. You can perhaps imagine how pleased the nomads were when they first tasted the sun-warmed sweetness of my fruit. To taste Oriental dates yourself, however, you will need a magic carpet. For by the time I reach you, I am either dried, with a slightly wrinkly skin and enormously sweet, or semi-dried— because even what is sold as fresh to you was frozen after the harvest. Bedouins and Berbers also value me dried, because I will keep for a long time, and they eat me in the morning with pot cheese on flatbread, just as you would eat butter and jam on toast. I come from a very large family, where some types can be made into bread and others into liquor. Cooks and bakers like to marry me with rice, poultry, lamb, and ground meat as well as marzipan, almonds, and cookies.

& Tea Coffee

Tea is for everyday, coffee for special days. Tea is essential, coffee is a luxury. What can I get you?

The Orient may be the home of coffee, yet it is tea which is much more at home here. Whether taken on a rug in a Bedouin tent, or at the stall of a spice trader in Marrakech, and even in your local kebab shop—everything always begins with some tea when they are authentically Oriental. To welcome a potential client in the bazaar, to close a deal in a restaurant, to start the day with bread, to round off dinner—tea is always present.

Tea sets the tone

The images we have of tea drinking are absent in the Middle East. The teapot is not made of porcelain; it is made of brightly polished metal, and sits on a samovar, or directly over a fire. The hot beverage is drunk from a glass, not a cup, and from Istanbul to Marrakech tea is so overwhelmingly sweet, that it will drive anyone mad who is obsessed with fashionable first-flush harvests. But tea in the Orient is not for people like that, despite all its associated rituals.

And what about coffee? What about mocha and Arabica? Did Islam forbid them in the same way as wine? No, not at all. In fact the mullahs praised them, since the caffeine with its side effects seemed to be an excellent replacement for the effects of the devilish alcohol. Indeed, following its discovery in Africa and its spread by the Yemenites in the 15th century, coffee soon became the national drink from the Caspian Sea to the Atlantic Ocean. Then, around 400 years ago, a few things happened all at the same time. In Persia, the rulers caught scent of a rebellion in the coffee houses, and they added Arabica to their list of forbidden items. But the caravans trading with Asia came with a worthy substitute in the form of tea leaves. This became the new Persian national drink, and it was soon adopted by the Ottomans.

The traders were very contented with this, especially the Europeans. Tea from far away opened up new and more lucrative markets

than were available for coffee, which was already present in the Middle East. (Today Iran and Turkey grow their own tea.) The Moroccans, for example, only became tea drinkers when England began to look for a new market for its imports from Asia. Today in the west of the Orient nothing is possible without Chinese green gunpowder tea, the basis for Moroccan mint tea. In other parts of the Middle East, black tea is the standard. In between, there are myriad varieties of tea flavored with blossom water, honey, aniseed and fennel seeds, marjoram, rosemary, saffron, or cinnamon. And some traditional teas have never even seen a tea leaf, because they are made from pieces of apple, hibiscus, or medicinal herbs.

Preparation in a Russian-Persian-Turkish samovar and in a Moroccan iron pot is robust—neither a first-flush Darjeeling nor a fine Japanese green tea is desirable. In Oriental stores you can find types for various different preparations as well as original Turkish tea; Iranian tea, on the other hand, is rare. There is, however, no reason not to stock up on black and green tea from a normal tea shop or from an organic health-food store. The general rule is: Cheap is rarely very good.

Coffee makes music

For the better moments in life in the Orient, there is coffee—the drink for holidays spent at home with the family and for relaxed afternoons at the coffee stand in the bazaar. Whoever tastes a Turkish "kahve" or mocha, or even a traditional Arabica, brewed in the embers, gets to feel the Orient in all its force and delights. The special roasting process, and the heating of a strong concoction of powder with sugar in the copper pot, make a mocha taste a little of caramel, a lot of coffee, and a little bit earthy. And it can go very quickly from earthy to muddy if you take that one sip too many, and get the grounds on your tongue. Now, as before, mystics will tip the grounds into their saucer and tell the future from the pattern they create.

In order to make an unfiltered mocha you will need very finely ground coffee of the Arabica variety. This can be found in a Turkish grocery store, as well as in all well-stocked supermarkets. Mocha connoisseurs swear that it is even more essential that the coffee be freshly ground when brewing a mocha in a pot, than when you are making an espresso. Ask at you local coffee store if they can grind Arabica for mocha. If they can, then they probably know what they are talking about and deserve your business in the future.

Oriental Basics:

Tea & Coffee

Black tea: Tea as it is drunk mainly in the east of the Orient, called "çay" in Turkish. Recipe page 94.

Mint tea: Black (in the east) or green (in the Mahgreb, especially in Morocco) tea, which is brewed and served with mint. Recipe page 36.

Gunpowder tea: Tea leaves which have shrunk into small balls like bullets as they dried. Existing as both black or green tea, the latter is typically used for Moroccan mint tea.

Apple tea: Turkish tea made from dried apples and lots of sugar, and drunk hot or cold. To serve 4–6 drinkers, let 5 tea-spoons of tea steep for 10 minutes in 1 quart of boiled water.

Karkadeh: Egyptian tea made from dried mallow or hibiscus blossoms. Characteristically bright red, it is sweetened with sugar or sugar syrup. Leave 2/3 ounce of blossoms to steep for 4 hours in 1 quart of cold water. Boil 1/4 cup of sugar with the same quantity of water. Strain the tea, mix with the sugar syrup, and leave to cool. Serve well chilled.

Samovar: Originally a Russian kettle for boiling water for tea. Initially it was heated with coals, today it may be heated electrically. A small pot on top of the samovar is used both for brewing tea and for diluting the tea. Mostly used in Turkey and Iran.

Kahve: The Turkish name for coffee, brewed with grounds in a can (which is called cezve or in Arabic canaka—see the almanac on the flap), often called mocha. Recipe page 58.

Where are you from...
...Arabica?

I am a mountain child—from the African mountains, the part where today Ethiopia is to be found. Apparently the people there initially brewed an invigorating or mildly intoxicating tea from my leaves, before they discovered the power of my red fruits and the coffee beans contained inside. A trading city in Yemen finally recognized my real value, imported me, and started my first plantation. From here I was initially sent to the rest of the Arab peninsula, from which my beautiful name "Arabica" is derived. Then I was taken up by the Ottomans, who brought me as far as the wide and wonderful world of Europe. There the dealers in Venice and the bakers in Vienna were the first to fall for my charms. A baker found me in sacks at the gates to his city, opened a coffee house with me, and created a cookie with me in the shape of the Islamic half moon, known as "Kipferl." But I am digressing—let me just say this: Outside of the Orient, it is the Venetians and Viennese who know how to get the best out of me. The Viennese call it "mocha"—after the port in Yemen to which I owe my worldwide fame.

Orient now !

The outside world and the Orient, that is a very long and a very old tale. It begins with Adam and Eve, whose Garden of Paradise is thought to have been somewhere near Baghdad; it reaches its exciting climax in Jerusalem, and there it also became a very sad and sorry tale in the end. This is, however, exactly what makes it all so interesting for so many people. In the following pages we will try to tell a little of this tale as we go. First we will follow a list of keywords which we are all familiar with: from the stories of the 1001 nights, from the Bible, and from our own experience in our everyday lives. Then we will explore the mysterious world of Oriental cuisine, which is generally only revealed to a privileged few. And finally we will, as strangers, knock on the door of an Oriental house, to leave again later as friends. All this will make us much wiser. Indeed, we will be wise enough to go into our own kitchens and cook genuine Oriental fare for ourselves. Bismillah!

17
secrets
of 1001 nights

Stories

I am a storyteller. I travel from bazaar to bazaar, unroll my carpet, and display my treasures: fairy-tales, parables, narratives, and sentimental stories. My sources come from your tents, villas, and kitchens; my material is your lives, loves, and quarrels. I will try to be an oasis for you. So put away your cooking spoon and pay attention to what happened a thousand years ago and more. Read, and laugh, and listen, and learn what has come about from all that. And later pay attention to the advice of the djin in the lamp, my wise friend and jester. But now let us begin—on to the **CARPET** we get.

Carpets

A real nomad always carries his home in his hand luggage. Woven from the wool of his sheep and goats, dyed with plants from along his way. The kilim, embroidered with all his family's information, once hung rolled on a camel's back, readily becomes a tent floor, a picnic blanket, a mattress, or a prayer mat. The Persians turned it into a work of art in velvet and silk, Aladdin made it fly, and today we can see them lying on tiled and wooden floors in our own homes. Just sit down on it cross-legged and drink a glass of tea—and the voyage begins, into the Oriental **HOUSE**.

Houses

Traditional Oriental houses, with their high windowless walls, look like the sand and stones which surround them, and from which they are built. A stronghold against the heat, curious onlookers, and enemies. Anyone, however, who is permitted to enter through a splendid gate as a friend will discover paradise: a light, tiled courtyard with a burbling fountain and shady greenery, from which colonnades lead to an artful interior. But do not venture too far, for you might end up in the private quarters. So let us just follow the host into the cool lobby and take a seat upon a **CUSHION**.

Cushions

When the carpet arrived in the Oriental home, it quickly became a cushion, upon which tea could be drunk in the traditional fashion, but without causing a cramp in the leg. The Persians spread cushions around their scriptorium for those who were waiting, and called them "diwan." This was transformed into a divan by the Ottomans—who fitted the cushions with legs, a piece of furniture that became widespread throughout the kingdom. From these "suffa" came our sofa, an Oriental invention, as is the mattress. But when the cushions are too nice, and the carpet too uncomfortable for a party, where do we put the food? On a **TRAY**.

Tray

Even before the sofa was invented in the Orient, the coffee table was already known: a tray—made from wood for everyday use, and from artfully hammered metal for special occasions—with short legs underneath or a folding frame. On this table were placed the ingredients for the tea ceremony, a rich selection of mezze, or a couscous from which you could help yourself. People who drop such a tray with both hands before their guests in true Oriental fashion, can hardly go wrong. They can then even get away with doing something that we have always considered very stuffy and old-fashioned. Read on under **SLIPPERS**.

Slippers

If your host opens the door in slippers, you usually can forget all about a wild and wicked party. The exception is an Oriental party. Here, wearing slippers is a must for all. Not, of course, old-fashioned felt slippers or sandals; only the originals from the Orient will do, pointed like the bell peppers in Turkey. They are known as cediks, babouche, or mules, and can be made of leather or the finest fabrics like silk, in either traditional or wildly colorful patterns and with delicate embroidery. They have come right back into fashion. And those in the know wear them on the street too—especially with baggy trousers at the market. Off to the **BAZAAR**.

Bazaar

Take a department store and a coffee shop, combine with circus tricks and crafts, sprinkle them around a mosque, and you have created a bazaar—"bazaar" in Persian, "suk" in Arabic, "market" in English. But what are words compared to the cries and the songs of the traders, the haggling and the hammering, the sizzling and the scents between the overflowing stalls. Although this chaos has its organization: Spices, silver pots, and plastic buckets each have their own alleyways. But what is one alleyway when there are hundreds? Keep calm; let us go to a coffee shop to enjoy a **HOOKAH**.

Hookah

We want neither to drug nor to poison, we want to tell a story. Like the Italian with his cafe, so the Oriental prefers the local coffee shop to his living room for a good smoke. Here the men sit at eye level with their shisha (Turkish shishe, Lebanese nargila), within which a piece of coal makes the tobacco smoke into a water tank. If you then suck on the pipe that is passed around, it forces the smoke to bubble through the water and flow chilled and filtered into your mouth. Harmful? Unhygienic? Sometimes even illegal? Perhaps, we only tell the tale. How about a little **GAME**?

Game

Chess comes from "Shah," the Persian king who gave his name to the world's best-known game. Invented in India, discovered by the Persians, it was the Arabs who made "the game of kings" popular in Europe from where it conquered the world. And more: Backgammon too comes from the playful Orient, where it was already played in ancient Babylon, and so does Kalaha, in which beans, marbles, or precious stones are made to hop through hollows. Even card games are supposed to have reached us from the Orient. You don't believe it? How about a little bet. I wager a **TREASURE**.

Treasures

What would the "Arabian Nights" have been without the treasure? As much as a bazaar without its artfully hammered pots and kettles, as much as a warrior without a sword of Damascus steel, as much as the richest woman of the kasbah without her jewelry—half as precious. While we were still making axes, artisans enriched the Orient with the finest in metalwork—treasures that winged the steps of fairy-tale heroes such as Sinbad and Ali Baba. The desert nomads, however, knew only one treasure: their livestock. Without them they had nothing. More about simple treasures under **STONE.**

Stone

The most amazing treasures were thought to be hidden behind rocks or in the sand—because it cannot be that life consists of sand and stone alone. The first houses were built from these, which made them almost invisible to enemies. Their greatest adversary, however, was the weather, from which tiles were supposed to offer protection, especially in corners and openings. These developed into magnificent ornaments and mosaics—superb treasures, as are the Oriental amphorae and faïences. All made of sand and stone. And concealed behind these is a real treasure—**WATER.**

Water

Those whose roots are in the desert require more water than others. Yet someone who has enough water there, becomes richer than anyone else. Like Egypt on the Nile, Baghdad between the Tigris and Euphrates, the ports on the gulf and the sea. Someone who must save water, will do so last before God. Here, washing is as much a religious duty as a visit to a hamam (public bath) is a luxury. And if there were a surplus of water, who would have thought of steaming couscous, slow-cooking tajines, or grilling lamb in a hole in the ground? There is more water to be found in an **OASIS.**

Oasis

The first oasis in the desert was Paradise: Those who were inside were forever happy, those who were outside had to fight to survive daily. The original oasis: When the desert released its water at a certain point then date palms and fig trees would immediately grow. And this is when the nomads arrived and were soon no longer nomads, first building houses, then city walls and fortresses. If the oasis was located on a trade route, riches and fame were as good as guaranteed; peace and quiet, however, were gone forever. Only a private oasis can help now, like a personal paradise. To find out more follow the **ROSE.**

17
secrets
of
1001 nights

Rose

English country ladies worship them as they do a cup of their best tea—but this is as nothing compared to the passionate love affair that has lasted thousands of years between the people of the Orient and the scent of the rose. The Persians were the first to cultivate them, and even today a "gulistan" (Persian for rose garden) in the middle of the desert is pure poetry. An oasis which is best hidden behind high walls, and so comes as an even greater surprise for guests. Those who do not have this can still spread rose petals and sprinkle them with rosewater, as is customary with a good host. Or make the flower into an **ORNAMENT.**

Ornament

No cherubs with puffed out cheeks, not even the Final Judgment—whoever enters a mosque will see no pictures. In their place will be seen splendidly flourishing patterns in all their glory and intricate detail. Even before the influence of Islam, Oriental artists and craftsmen concentrated more on delightfully repeating patterns than on brilliant and outstanding individual pieces. Their arabesques cover walls, columns, tiled floors, weapon handles, as well as books and found their way into calligraphic writing, and even onto hands in the form of henna paintings. Which brings us to **COLOR.**

Color

The Orient brought color into the desert and introduced it into our lives—historically, linguistically, and actually: yellow (originally won from saffron and turmeric); lilac (comes from "lilak," the Persian word for the lilac shrub); crimson (made by the Phoenicians from slugs); carmine (made by the Persians from lice); orange (originally made from the North African dyer thistle—the name comes from "naranji," the Persian word for the fruit); green (the color of Islam, historically made from verdigris); turquoise (this color cools even when you just look at it). More colors in the **LIGHT.**

Light

"Ex oriente lux," it was said in Latin, "from the East comes the light." Because it is there that the sun rises. Because it is there that the moon rules the calendar. Because it is there that astronomy was founded. Because it is there that Christians, Jews, and Muslims see the birthplace of their religions. Because Oriental traders and scientists brought light to darkest Europe. Because there are fires, large and small, over and over again. Because it is there that we read about the magical oil lamp, from which Aladdin awakened the good djin in the Arabian Nights. Now we're back to **STORIES.** More?

In the kitchen

The kitchen is one of the most mysterious places in the Orient. Secretly, small and great miracles are accomplished here, things that should no longer be possible if you are a modern person. Luckily we are not.

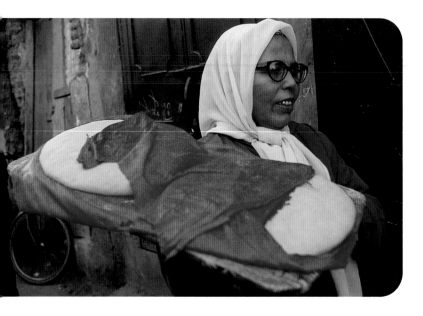

The sun rises in the East...

The desert outside still lies cold and gray in the last hour of the night, the dew still captures the scent of the rose garden, the TV screens are still blank, and the muezzin silent. The devout among the men prepare themselves in their booths for the first prayer, the women slowly take control of the kitchens. The day before they had already kneaded the dough for the flatbread, which they now roll once more, then press flat, and slide onto a board. One of the daughters arrives, the first words pass, the day begins to unfold. A youth takes the board and carries it through the alleyways that are beginning to flood with sunlight to the baker. The chat and the gossip of the others can be heard from a few blocks away, the chat of those waiting for "their" bread to reappear from the red-hot oven. And as every morning, they carry back the freshly baked bread, wrapped in a cloth, to the house where the family is ready and waiting for the first breakfast.

On a day like today...

It sounds like the fairy-tale of 1001 mornings, and to really experience such a morning, you would have to be in a small village in the countryside. The bread dough might also be taken to the bakery later, after the family has gathered strength from a thick soup made from beans or other legumes and cereals. In the towns and less traditional areas we feel more at home, starting with the pace of life, where, if the mother also works, there is little time for traditional duties. But we know all this. And in this book we want to learn about things we do not know. So we shall follow the day in the kitchen of a traditional Oriental family a little further. At this point we must admit that we are going on hearsay. This is because there is no place for strangers in these Oriental kitchens, especially for men—with the exception of young boys, who are not yet men. For sons too, the time comes when as a teenager they must stay in the public area, where the guests are, where the mint tea is brewed, and where Dad is sometimes allowed to grill some kebabs. So much the better then if as a boy he paid close attention in the kitchen.

The basics for an Oriental breakfast are bread, cheese, pickles such as olives, fresh products such as tomatoes or cucumbers, and sweet foods such as dates or honey. In certain regions there could also be a thick soup or, as in Egypt, cooked and dressed beans (recipe page 90). Sometimes bread will be dunked in olive oil with herbs or sprinkled with dukkah (a mixture of spices, nuts, and seeds). In Turkey reçel, a sort of marmalade, is commonly found on the breakfast table, and in Morocco they adore beghir, fluffy pancakes with holes than can be drenched and dripping with butter and honey. To drink there is mostly tea—black, green, with or without mint—and rarely mocha coffee, and much rarer still Arabian coffee.

All the time in the world...

When it is exceptionally hot at midday, or when the family has been at different places during the day, lunch is not taken too seriously. A few mezze, or a quick meal with bread, some spicy scrambled eggs perhaps. Or you buy falafel, kebabs, or stuffed bread from a street vender. If there is something to celebrate, or if the family is particularly status conscious, a traditional lunch will be served with a variety of hot and cold dishes for many—something that is otherwise reserved for the evening. At any rate cooking starts early, as a pan of beans, or some half-cooked, half-steamed Persian rice, or especially a traditionally prepared couscous, can take hours to reach perfection.

Let us stay with couscous. We heard of a woman in Marrakesh who does not fit the traditional image of an Oriental woman. She is a businesswoman, she runs a company that produces rosewater. She has few children, and she taught her son, who is married to a French woman and lives in Germany, how to cook. This is quite unusual. And yet, she still dries her spices in the traditional way on the flat roof of her house, into which she would never admit a packet of instant couscous. This presteamed and fast-swelling semolina has become a standard item for us in the west, even in Oriental stores. Only organic food stores and specialty delicatessens here still stock the traditional couscous with which our Moroccan mother cooks.

This takes place most typically on Fridays, the Islamic "Sunday." Then the semolina grains simmer in a special couscousière, which has a steaming colander-like insert—just like our double steamers—that contains the couscous and hangs suspended above the hot and steaming stew. After a ritual which takes several hours of steaming, emptying, rinsing, stirring, seasoning, and fine-tuning, the couscous will emerge light, fluffy, perfumed, and filled with aroma. Ready to be heaped up and spread out to a flattened cone, to be surrounded by stew, and to be served and enjoyed.

In the Orient, the cook takes all the time in the world in the kitchen, in order for the spices to reveal and blend their flavors, and for each morsel to become tender enough to be eaten later by hand. Over many hours, days, and years the cook develops the knowledge about which spice should be added where and when, and how a well-made dough should feel. These women are also professionals at the bazaar, where they go early to purchase the vegetables, herbs, and fruits for their meals. They would like to teach their daughters (exceptions prove the rule) to acquire the same feeling for food in each finger of their right hands. Even if the daughter would not dream of spending half her life in the kitchen like her mother—at this moment she is there, and so she happily picks parsley, grates tomatoes into a sauce, and grinds cumin and garlic in pestle and mortar for all the mezze and marinades.

Let us celebrate...

When a large celebration approaches, the woman of the house receives plenty of female reinforcements days before the event. Grandmothers, aunts, cousins, woman friends, all come to help, and each one does what she does best. What that is, is of course not necessarily something that can be agreed upon, and so there is much occasion for discussing, tasting, criticizing, and laughing, until somehow eventually all the bowls, dishes, and platters are ready and groaning with delicacies, and concealing every square inch of the tablecloth. One thing is certain: There must always be plenty—and more than enough for the guests—and what there is must be of the highest quality that you can afford. There is at any rate lots of meat and fish, something rather more rarely seen on the table in everyday life. Lamb, sometimes mutton, and poultry are important, beef and veal more unusual, and, of course, there is no pork—for Muslims, as with Jews. The meat, whether stewed in the tajine or grilled on a skewer, is always well cooked, preferably until it is so tender that it will just fall apart and can easily be eaten with the fingers. Fish are usually grilled whole: for example, barbels or sardines. Seafood, though, is considered "haram" or "taboo" for Muslims (and again as for Jews) because the creatures swim but have no scales.

The guest

Everything is done for guests in the Orient. The fortress becomes an open house, the hut becomes a palace. Strangers are made friends, enemies are now brothers. And the most important ingredient in this hospitality is a friendly guest.

We knock...

And so we are standing in front of this house, in which the bread dough was kneaded this morning, where immediately afterwards the couscous was set to cook in the traditional manner, so that the whole family can eat at lunchtime. We shall join them today as guests. The high wall along the alley is a brilliant white. In front of us on the corner, the branch of a date palm waves over the roof terrace, and the scent of oranges wafts over us. The wooden gate is fitted in an arch the height of a man, both wings painted a rich green and fitted with shining metal mounts. Before us, hung on the hinge, is a bronze hand whose fingers clasp a ball the size of an apricot. It is shiny, polished by the hands of the guests who reach for it daily. We knock.

My friend, the guest...

Yes, we are dreaming again. First of the women's kitchens, and now of a grand Oriental mansion. And yes, we can accept that for some this may sound more like a nightmare from a long forgotten past. If this is the case, they also need to understand that perhaps they should not follow us any further. He who passes this door should fall into line. Behind it is a whole other world, to which we have been invited, and the inhabitants of this world will do everything to make us feel welcome, as though we were really in a palace while at their home. They will know how to create this impression even if they live in a hut. We have arrived.

As we have some experience, we did not arrive "on time," since no one would have expected us to. It could even be interpreted as impoliteness, since it ruins the Oriental planned hospitality. Nobody knows this plan, by which everything should run so as to be able to say afterward that Allah would have wanted it that way. He would want one thing for certain—He even had it noted in the Koran: That every guest, whether expected, punctual, polite, related, known or not, should be

allowed to enter your house as a "friend of Allah," and that you should offer him everything you have—and more. The guest who cries out his "open sesame" with tolerance and humility will see the fortress with its closed family unit suddenly become an open house. In this way, the descendants of the nomads have easily made friends, in an environment where they needed them—and did not create more enemies than they already had.

After you...

We enter, are warmly greeted by the man of the house (embracing is reserved for very close friends only), the children are hiding behind the fountain in the courtyard (and certainly we have brought something for them). The older sons will also welcome us (of course the eldest first). The lady of the house may also be present, depending on how traditionally the family lives—we will let her decide (and we will most certainly not embrace her). While we ask after the family, and in return tell of our country (only good things!), we move slowly toward the divan, the reception lobby, where a table tray with an embroidered tablecloth awaits us, surrounded by cushions. The host offers us his best places, which we offer back to him, which he then refuses, until finally we are all agreed. Unless the game begins all over again: Who will be seated first? This ritual may be repeated frequently. The rule of thumb: Finally, after three back and forths, you should accept, so that the host has his way and you have meanwhile demonstrated your politeness, and so that everyone can move on.

To get in the mood some drinks and snacks are passed around, and the host will often like to deal with the tea or coffee himself. We sit around the table with the soles of our feet hidden from view—the men cross-legged, the women sitting on their (covered) legs. For important guests and relations, the wife can also be present, as long as everything in the kitchen is in hand. Otherwise,

Enjoy your meal...

The meal is begun by the man of the house with a "Bismillah" (Our Father), which is repeated by all. He then breaks the bread and passes it first to the guests. From then on everyone helps themselves. There may be a spoon, or perhaps even a fork and a plate for foreign guests. Otherwise, bread is cutlery and plate in one, with which the foods are taken directly from the platter (for more information see page 14). If there is only one large platter in the center of the table, each person must be careful not to stray into another's area. If there are many dishes on the table, the host will make sure that what he thinks is the best is near his guests—even then, one only eats what is nearest. Even if other dishes are provided, we should eat the most of those dishes the host had chosen for us—while leaving sufficient room for the others. If we eat from a plate, the lady of the house will make sure that it is never empty. The only way to overcome this is to leave something on your plate and, despite pleading, stick to a friendly "no." But beware: The others will stop eating as soon as the guest does. It is useful to know that in the Middle East people usually eat quickly and quietly.

Once fresh fruit or one of the rare desserts has been consumed, the host will rise from table with a "Hamdulillah" (Thank Allah). It is usual then to move to another place to chat over tea, mocha, and sweet biscuits for as long as you desire. However: Before the guest decides to leave, even the most exhausted host will act as if they could go on for hours. And at the first sign of departure, the well-known game of back and forth will begin again: the request to stay, the lengthy thanks for all that has been done—it is best therefore to begin the ritual early enough to allow both sides to part fully satisfied. The easiest trick here, is to place yourself in the shoes (or slippers) of the host before doing or saying anything. And with that we have reached the next stage of hospitality—the return invitation. This is a must, even if it is clear that it will never actually happen.

And so we thank you for your attention up to now, and would like to invite you on, to the next page, to share in the Orient's cooking secrets. Inshallah.

she will deal with the cooking herself, and take her meal separately with the other women of the household. Western women, by the way, are generally treated in the same way as men.

It is very important to wash your hands before eating—for religious and practical reasons since food is often eaten by hand from one communal platter. Traditionally a pitcher of perfumed water is passed around the diners for washing hands over a bowl; otherwise it is off to the sink as usual. And then it begins. Following the ancient tradition everything prepared in the kitchen is placed on the table, and that is far more than anyone could ever possibly eat, however large their appetite. Normally cold and warm dishes are served separately. We start with the appetizers—mezze, salads, dips—and then, depending on the occasion, one or more bowls of hot delicacies will be placed on the table. Bread is always present, throughout the meal, and often there are bowls of spices and herbs as well as pieces of vegetables to be chewed in between.

The Recipes

Snacks &

Help yourself to these tasy morsels

Salads

"Welcome to our humble home. It would give us great pleasure to share our bread and cheese with you." What a fantastic greeting! And these are only passersby who just wanted to take a quick peek at an Oriental home—which is, of course, not as easy as it sounds.

"Some mint tea? No, of course it's no trouble at all. Who knows when we will meet again. And you absolutely must try these pistachios. They're fresh, sent by my cousin in Isfahan. What, you also have a cousin there? Well, well, I wouldn't be at all surprised..." What follows is a lengthy exchange on whether host and guest might have friends or even relatives in common in the wide lands of the Orient... We'll forget about that for now.

"Ah, here come the mezze [appetizers], thank you, my dear wife. Please help yourselves, help yourselves. Magical, you say? You'd like to know how they're made? Well, of course, normally a magician doesn't explain his tricks. But since I noticed right away that you have an appreciation of the good things in life and since we are virtually related, I'll make an exception for this once. Open Sesame!" And now please turn the page.

What the Orient drinks
Mint Tea

The farther west the caravan treks across the desert, the mintier and lighter in color is the Oriental tea. In Morocco, finally, it is a sweet, refreshing brew made from green tea and plenty of fresh mint that is poured into the tea glass at every opportunity and with a lot of panache. This aeration helps intensify the flavor and stops it scalding your lips. The best tea to use is green "gunpowder tea," whose leaves shrivel into tiny pellets while drying. You can find it on gourmet shelves and in Asian grocery stores, but if you can't find it, you can use any other pungent green tea instead.

To make 4 small glasses, pour a little boiling water over 3 teaspoons of gunpowder tea, leave to steep, then strain after 1 minute. Put the swollen tea leaves into a saucepan, together with 4 teaspoons sugar and 4 stalks aromatic mint (Moroccan nana mint is best, but never use peppermint). Pour over 1 cup hot water. Cover and simmer very gently for 10 minutes. If you own one of those attractive Oriental metal teapots with small feet and a domed lid, make the tea straight in the pot. If not, just transfer everything from the saucepan into an ordinary teapot.

Now pour the tea into a glass (it's OK for a stalk of mint to remain in the glass), while lifting the pot high up into the air with a flourish so that the tea you pour starts foaming. If it splashes instead, you'll need to practice a little more. But we have lots of time...

1001
Nights...

... are enchanting

"Ali Baba and the Forty Thieves," this is the title of one of the 1001 tales that were once told to the King of the Sassanids, night after night, by Sheharazade, the vizier's daughter. The reasons were not exactly enchanting. The king had been deceived by his wife. As a punishment, she was beheaded. And so was every "woman for one night" that the vizier brought to the king afterwards. That's until it was the vizier's own daughter's turn, and she started telling her stories. 1001 nights later she was still alive, and soon she became the new queen. And they lived happily ever after...

It is from this framework tale that 1001 legends, fables, and parables were combined in the most famous collection of the Orient, *Alf laila wa-laila*. It became famous around the world with the 18th-century French translation, *Les mille et une nuits*. In the U.S.A. it is known as *The Book of One Thousand and One Nights* or *Arabian Nights*. Like the Grimms' fairytales, the collection comprises stories from various cultures, ranging from Persia, India, Greece, Egypt, Arabia, and Mesopotamia to Turkey. As is to be expected in Oriental tales, sensual pleasures loom large: "She bought apples of the purest color, peaches from Khoullane, limes from Marakib, the most exquisite cedrat lemons." At some point the writer enthuses about "pistachio nuts—a crunchy pleasure while drinking in good company—raisins from Chib, dates from Iraq." Another time he praises "butter beignets, wafer-thin pancakes, musk pies, Turkish caramel." What does it mean? In the Orient, pleasure and pain are closely entwined. People here really seem to know how to enjoy life—or do you know of any comparable passages in the Grimms' fairy-tales?

About visiting

Generous Genie!

This is Magical!.
You granted me my wish
to visit your homeland.
And traveling by
carpet is so very
comfortable.
Thank you, too,
for announcing
my visit to
your friend.
But tell me:
What should
I do now?

First of all know this: You will always be welcome. Really always. And if you are a traveler lacking in food, or drink, or a bed for the night, then my friend will give you all these things as a matter of course. And he will always give more than he keeps for himself. For there must never be too little for a guest, and nothing can ever be too expensive. Therefore, enter his home with humility. Imagine yourself as a host, especially if you request something from him. And then be humble and silent. Your every wish will be fulfilled anyway.

First of all, greet your host with open arms, shaking hands, and wishing him "salamaleikum." Express genuine interest as you ask after the wellbeing of his family and his children. Then greet all the older men in the house, making sure to ask each about their health. If you wish to carry a gift, do not bring any flowers for the lady of the house, and definitely do not bring any wine. Better bets are candy and small gifts for the children. Why not take something strange and beautiful from your own country? Shall I magic something up for you?

Home-made Oriental Basics

Dukkah

In Egypt, this roughly crushed mixture of seeds, grains, and spices is often served with flat bread for breakfast. You may think it looks a bit like bird food. Try it. Grab a fresh piece of bread, dunk it in the finest olive oil, and then dip it in the dukkah—you'll love this "bird food." Now it is often served as an aperitif snack in fashionable bars and restaurants, and not just in Oriental ones. And you can also sprinkle it over soups and salads. This is how to make it:

Boil 1 cup hazelnut kernels in water for 5 minutes, then put through a strainer and leave to cool. The skin is now easily removed by rubbing the kernels between your fingers. Combine the nuts with 1 cup sesame seeds as well as 5 tablespoons each of cilantro and cumin seeds. Sprinkle the mixture onto a cookie sheet. Place the sheet in the center of a preheated oven at 480 °F for a good 5 minutes, until all the seeds are toasted and release their aromatic scent. Don't let them get too dark. Remove the seed mixture from the sheet. Leave to cool. Season with pepper and salt, then roughly crush the mixture with a pestle and mortar or grind it in a blender. Do not reduce it to a powder or paste. And now get dipping!

What does it mean...
...Open, Sesame?

The story of "Ali Baba and the Forty Thieves" is probably the best known of the *Tales of 1001 Nights*. It's so famous that there are western versions of the tale. It always includes a magic command used by the poor woodcutter Ali Baba to get into the robbers' den and to reach their gold: "Open, Sesame." But why sesame? Before olive oil and sunflower oil were discovered in the Orient, sesame oil was the most important oil in the kitchen. It was used in oil lamps too. At the time, sesame was planted on a large scale. The seeds were harvested when they were still unripe because at this stage they contained the most oil. You could, however, only collect the oil when the valuable seeds started dropping out of their pods as they were drying—and this sometimes took a very long time. And so everyone could understand what the impatient Ali Baba must have felt when he stood in front of the closed den, and why he uttered his magical command: "Open, Sesame."

Babaganoush
The star among appetizers

Serves 4:

2 smallish eggplants (about 1 pound

3 tablespoons sesame paste (tahini)

3 tablespoons lemon juice

2 tablespoons olive oil

2 garlic cloves

salt

freshly ground black pepper

1/2 bunch parsley (flat-leaved if available)

1 tablespoon black olives

1 Heat the oven to 475 °F. Wash the egg-plants and prick them a few times with a sharp knife. Bake on a tray in the center of the oven for about 30 minutes, or until a knife is easily inserted and the skin is almost black.

2 Remove the eggplants from the oven and leave to cool until easy to handle. Slice open lengthwise and scoop out the soft flesh with a spoon. Put it into a blender, together with the sesame paste, lemon juice, and olive oil, and purée to a smooth paste.

3 Peel the garlic, crush, and mix well into the purée. Season with salt and pepper. Wash the parsley and shake it dry. Pull off and finely chop the leaves. Scatter over the purée together with the olives.

Time you need: 15 minutes
(+ 30 minutes baking)
Goes well with: flatbread
Calories per portion: 140

Variations:

Eggplant purée with tomatoes

Bake the eggplants as described and scoop out the flesh. Chop finely, but do not purée. Wash, trim, and/or peel 2 tomatoes, 2 chilis, 1 onion, and 2 garlic cloves. Chop everything finely and combine with the eggplants. Stir in 2–3 tablespoons lemon juice, 2 tablespoons olive oil, salt, and 1 pinch sugar. Check the seasoning. Serve with bread.

Eggplant purée with pomegranates

Bake the eggplants as described and scoop out the flesh. Purée in a blender, mix in 3 tablespoons pomegranate syrup (also known as grenadine) and 3 tablespoons olive oil. Peel and crush 2 garlic cloves and add. Wash, shake dry, and chop finely half the parsley. Stir it into the purée. Season well with salt and pepper, and transfer to a bowl. Remove the seeds from half a pomegranate (break it into chunks and remove the seeds with your fingers) and scatter the seeds over the eggplant purée.

Eggplant purée with yogurt

Bake the eggplants as described and scoop out the flesh. Purée in a blender. Grate, break into very small pieces or chop finely 1 cup walnut kernels. Dry-roast in a skillet until they release a scent. Leave to cool, then stir into the eggplant purée together with 2/3 cup yogurt. Season with 1 teaspoon each of sumac, salt, pepper, and sweet paprika. Take just the green parts from 2 scallions. Wash and cut into thin rings. Scatter the green rings over the eggplant purée, then sprinkle lightly with paprika.

Paprika and walnut paste
Red, spicy, good

Serves 4:

3 red bell pepppers

1/2 cup yogurt (set sheep milk yogurt is best)

1 cup shelled walnuts

1 cup one-day old bread

2 tablespoons butter

2 garlic cloves

salt

1 teaspoon harissa (see p.95)

1/2 bunch parsley

1 Preheat the oven to 480 °F (if you have a convection oven, also preheat this now to 420 °F). Wash the red pepppers and halve lengthwise, cutting through the stem ends if necessary. Remove the stems, the white membranes, and the seeds. Place the peppers skin side up on a cookie sheet (covered first with parchment paper if possible) and bake in the center of the oven for about 15 minutes, or until the skin starts to blister and turn black.

2 In the meantime, spoon the yogurt into a fine strainer and leave to drain. When the peppers are baked, remove them from the oven and leave to cool until you can handle them. (Extra tip: Place a damp cloth over the peppers or place them in a plastic bag, and the skin will be even easier to remove.) Skin the peppers when they are no longer too hot to hold. This will be easy in some places, more difficult in others. It doesn't matter if a few bits of skin stay on the flesh.

3 Finely grate the walnuts and the bread in a food processor. Put the butter into a skillet and melt over a medium heat. Add the nuts and the breadcrumbs and fry for 2–3 minutes in the butter, stirring all the time so that they don't burn. Remove from the skillet as soon as they start to turn brown.

4 Peel and roughly chop the garlic, then purée it together with the red peppers to a fine consistency. Stir in the yogurt and the nut mixture. Season the paste to taste with salt and harissa. Try a little spoonful. Is it sufficiently fiery? Adjust seasoning, then spoon the paste into a bowl. Wash the parsley and shake it dry. Pull off the leaves and use to garnish the paste. All done!

Time you need: 35 minutes
Goes well with: flatbread
Calories per portion: 275

Speedy version:

Don't bother baking and skinning the peppers, just process them raw with the nuts and the bread. For this speedy version, don't add any yogurt—it would make the paste too sloppy and liquid.

Fiery pepper salsa

Known as "zhug," this kicks a real punch

Serves 4:

1 green bell pepper

6 green chilis

8 garlic cloves

4 green cardamom pods

1 bunch cilantro

1 teaspoon ground cumin

salt

1 Wash the bell pepper, halve it lengthwise, remove stem, white membranes, and seeds. Dice the flesh. Wash the chilis and slit them open lengthwise, remove stems and seeds. Peel and roughly chop the garlic cloves. Crack open the cardamom pods and remove the seeds.

2 In an electric blender, purée the pepper, chilis, garlic cloves, and cardamom seeds to a smooth paste.

3 Wash the cilantro and shake it dry. Pull off the leaves, add them to the paste and stir them in. Season the salsa to taste with cumin and salt.

Time you need: 25 minutes
Goes well with: falafel (page 68) and shish kebab (page 124), flatbread, and grilled vegetables; the salsa can also be used to flavor soups and meat dishes
Calories per portion: 20

Or try this:

Vary the colors and use red bell peppers and red chilis instead. Flavor with a little lemon juice and honey.

Hummus

An absolute must on a platter of appetizers

Serves 4:

1 can garbanzos (14 ounces appprox.)

2 garlic cloves

2 tablespoons olive oil

3 tablespoons lemon juice

3 tablespoons sesame paste (tahini)

salt

1/2 teaspoon ground cumin

1 tablespoon butter

1 teaspoon sweet paprika

1 Thoroughly wash the garbanzos in a colander, then leave to drain. Peel and chop the garlic cloves.

2 Using an electric blender or food processor, purée the garbanzos, garlic, olive oil, lemon juice, 2–3 tablespoons water, and the tahini until you have a creamy paste. Season to taste with salt and cumin, then transfer into a small bowl. In the center of the paste make a hollow with a spoon.

3 Over a low heat, melt the butter in a small skillet; don't allow it to brown. Stir in the paprika. Pour the red butter into the hollow over the hummus.

Time you need: 10 minutes
Goes well with: pita bread and olives
Calories per portion: 220

"Not-in-a-rush" version:

The hummus will taste maybe just that tiny bit better—although not hugely so—if you use dried garbanzos. Over night, soak 2/3 cup dried garbanzos in water. The next day, change the water and cook the beans until they are soft. This takes 1–1 1/2 hours, depending on the age of the garbanzos. Continue as described above.

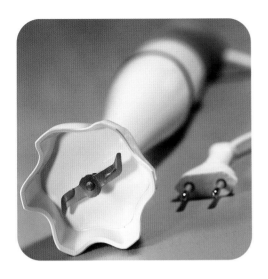

Variations:

Avocado hummus
Halve 2 nicely ripe avocados and remove the pit with the tip of the knife. Remove the flesh from the skins and finely purée it with 6 tablespoons lemon juice and 4 tablespoons sesame paste (tahini). Peel and crush 2 garlic cloves. Wash and shake dry a few stalks of parsley. Pull off the leaves, finely chop them, and stir them into the paste. Season to taste with 1 teaspoon ground cumin, salt, and 1/2 teaspoon harissa (page 95). Serve with hot flatbread and sliced tomatoes.

Fava
Leave 1 cup dried fava beans to soak over night in cold water. The following day, bring to a boil with 1 peeled and halved onion and simmer for about 1 hour until softened. Leave to cool a little, then pop the beans out of their skins. Purée with the onion, 2 peeled garlic cloves, 2 tablespoons olive oil, and 3 tablespoons lemon juice until smooth. Season to taste with salt, pepper, and a little sugar. Wash 1 bunch dill and shake dry, then finely chop and stir in. The fava paste tastes delicious with flatbreads and olives.

Feta cheese dip
A quickly prepared
Turkish delicacy

Serves 4:

4 ounces feta cheese

1/2 cup yogurt

1 large bunch parsley

1 bunch cilantro, 1 garlic clove

ground pepper

1 Crumble the feta cheese, then purée in the blender with the yogurt until smooth.

2 Wash herbs and shake dry. Pull off and finely chop leaves. Peel and crush garlic. Stir herbs and garlic into the paste, season with pepper. Don't add salt as the cheese is salty.

Time you need: 10 minutes
Goes well with: flatbread, sliced tomatoes, and cucumber
Calories per portion: 135

Or try this:
Stir 1 skinned red bell pepper (for how to skin them, see page 39) and 1 finely diced chili into the dip.

Carrot purée
Good for
the piggy bank

Serves 4:

1 pound carrots, salt

2 garlic cloves

2 tablespoons lemon juice

1 teaspoon ground cumin

1 teaspoon harissa (page 95)

2 tablespoons black olives

2 tablespoons olive oil

1 Peel carrots and cut them into 3/4 inch pieces. Put in a saucepan with the salt, cover with 3/4 inch water and bring to a boil. Cover with the lid, then cook carrots over a medium heat for about 20 minutes, or until soft.

2 Drain the carrots, leave to cool, then purée. Peel and crush the garlic and stir in. Stir the lemon juice, cumin, and harissa into the purée, season with salt.

3 Transfer the carrot purée to a bowl and garnish with the olives. Drizzle the oil on top.

Time you need: 30 minutes
Goes well with: flatbread
Calories per portion: 85

Parsley and spinach salad
Refreshingly spicy

Serves 4 as

an appetizer or a side dish:

1 pound spinach

salt

2 bunches parsley

3 garlic cloves

1/2 organic lemon

1 tablespoon green pitted olives

4 tablespoons olive oil

1/2 tablespoon each sweet paprika

and ground cumin

lemon wedges, to garnish

1 Fill the sink with cold water. Drop in the spinach and swish it around thoroughly. Drain in a colander. If the water has turned very sandy, wash the spinach again in fresh water. Discard all yellow and wilted leaves.

2 In a saucepan, bring about 2 pints salted water to a boil. Add the spinach to the saucepan, and push it under the water with a wooden spoon. Cook the spinach for about 1–2 minutes, until the leaves start to wilt.

Drain in a colander, refresh with plenty of cold water, then leave to drain well. Using your hands, gently squeeze a little more water from the leaves without bruising them too much. Now finely chop the spinach using a sharp knife.

3 Wash the parsley, shake it dry, then pull off the leaves and chop very finely. Peel and very finely chop the garlic. Brush the lemon under hot water, then thinly pare off the zest so that none of the white membrane comes off with it. Very finely chop the lemon zest. Now pare off the white membrane from the lemon flesh and discard it. Cut the lemon flesh into small dice, removing all the seeds as you do so. Chop the olives or cut them into thin strips.

4 Put the spinach, parsley, garlic, lemon zest and diced flesh, and the olives into a bowl and stir well to combine. In a small tumbler, combine the olive oil with the paprika, cumin, and salt and pour over the salad mixture. Stir very well again, and check for seasoning. You may want to add a little more salt. Garnish the salad with the lemon wedges, then take it to the table.

Time you need: 25 minutes
Goes well with: flatbread or sesame rings (page 61)
Calories per portion: 115

Or try this:
Instead of the lemon zest and flesh, use 1/2 pickled lemon (page 131). Wash under cold water, then cut the zest into very small pieces and stir into the salad. In this case, do not use the flesh of the lemons.

Spinach and yogurt
Creamy and mild

Serves 4:

1 pound spinach

1 large onion

2 tablespoons olive oil

2 teaspoons ground turmeric or

1/2 teaspoon ground saffron

salt, ground pepper

2 garlic cloves

1 1/3 cups yogurt

1 Thoroughly wash the spinach as described in the previous recipe. Discard all yellowing leaves. Pile the spinach leaves onto a cutting board, and chop with a large kitchen knife. Peel and halve the onion. Slice, then finely dice the onion.

2 Place a wide saucepan on the stove, add the oil, and heat it over a low flame. Stir in the diced onion and fry over a medium heat for about 5 minutes, stirring occasionally. Sprinkle in the turmeric or saffron and continue stirring until the onions are nicely golden. Add the spinach to the pan and continue stirring until it starts to wilt. Cover with the lid and simmer over a low heat for another 2–3 minutes.

3 Transfer the spinach to a bowl and season with salt and pepper. Leave to cool. Peel the garlic, crush it into the yogurt and stir well. Stir the yogurt into the spinach. Check for seasoning and adjust with salt and pepper if necessary.

Time you need: 25 minutes
Goes well with: pita bread with sumac (page 61) or sesame sticks
Calories per portion: 115

Or try this:
Stir 2–3 tablespoons ground walnuts into the yogurt. Alternatively, dry-roast the nuts and sprinkle them over at the end. Or cut the ends off 1 stalk celery, pull off the strings if necessary. Wash celery and cut into thin slices. Combine with the cooked spinach.

Cucumber yogurt with raisins
Unusual and sweet

Serves 4:

1/4 cup raisins

1/3 cup shelled walnuts

1/2 bunch mint

1 smallish cucumber

1 3/4 cups yogurt

salt, ground pepper

1 Wash the raisins in a strainer under hot water and leave to drain well. Very finely chop the walnut kernels.

2 Wash the mint and shake it dry. Pull off and finely chop the leaves. Peel the cucumber, then halve it lengthwise. Scrape out the seeds with a spoon. Finely chop the cucumber flesh.

3 Put the yogurt into a bowl, and season with salt and pepper. Stir in the raisins, walnuts, mint, and cucumber. Chill yogurt in the fridge for about 1 hour. Stir again and taste-test. Do you need to adjust the seasoning with a little salt and pepper? Do so, then quickly get the dish to the table.

Time you need: 15 minutes
(+ 1 hour chilling)
Goes well with: grilled vegetables and flatbread, but also delicious with grilled or broiled lamb chops
Calories per portion: 190

Or try this:
Stir some finely chopped prunes or dates into the cucumber yogurt. Or just leave out the fruits and nuts, and season the yogurt instead with some crushed garlic.

Variation:

Carrot yogurt with dill
Peel and finely grate 3 carrots. Heat 1 tablespoon butter and 1 tablespoon olive oil and gently sweat the carrots in this for 2–3 minutes, stirring all the time. Transfer the carrots to a bowl and leave to cool. Wash and shake dry 1 bunch dill. Pinch off and discard the thickest stalks, then finely chop the rest together with 2 peeled garlic cloves. Stir into the carrots together with 1 3/4 cups yogurt, Season with salt, pepper, and 1/2 teaspoon hot paprika.

Roasted bell peppers
An old favorite with a new marinade

Serves 4:

4 nice fat red bell peppers

1/2 organic lemon

1/2 bunch parsley

1 chili, 2 teaspoons cuminseeds

salt, ground pepper

1 pinch sweet paprika

4 tablespoons olive oil

1 Preheat the oven to 450 °F (convection oven also now to 425 °F). Line a baking tray with foil or parchment paper.

2 Halve the bell peppers lengthwise. Remove the stems, seeds, and white membranes. Place the peppers skin side up onto the baking trays. Bake in the oven (center) for about 15 minutes, until the skin bubbles up in large, black blisters.

44

3 Take the peppers out of the oven and leave to cool until you can touch them. Pull off as much of the skin as possible. Cut the flesh of the peppers into strips and place these on a platter or a large plate.

4 Brush the lemon half under hot water. Thinly pare off the zest, leaving all the bitter white pith behind. Cut the zest into very thin strips. Squeeze out the lemon juice. Wash and shake dry the parsley. Pull off the leaves and finely chop them. Wash the chili, slit open lengthwise, and remove the stem end. Depending on how hot you like your food, leave the seeds in or remove them. (If you use your fingers to remove the seeds, make sure you wash your hands carefully and avoid touching your eyes.) Cut the chili halves into thin strips.

5 Heat up a small skillet, and dry-roast the cumin seeds. Pour them into a mortar and crush lightly with the pestle. Combine the lemon juice with the cumin, salt, pepper, and paprika, and stir well to mix. With a fork, beat in the oil, a few drops at a time. Sprinkle the lemon zest, parsley, and chili over the pepper strips, then drizzle over the sauce. Leave to marinate for at least 1 hour.

Time you need: 40 minutes
(+ 1 hour marinating)
Goes well with: flatbread
Calories per portion: 125

Variation:

Bell peppers with pickled lemons
Skin, then dice the peppers. Peel and finely chop 2 garlic cloves, and combine with parsley, chili, and the diced peppers. Make a dressing from lemon juice, 2 teaspoons ground cumin, and olive oil. Instead of the lemon zest, use 1/2 pickled lemon (page 131). Wash it, cut off the zest, and finely chop it. Combine with the diced peppers, and stir in the dressing. Season with salt and pepper, and leave to marinate for a while.

Saffron onions with honey
Simply irresistible

Serves 4:

1 pound small onions (flattish onions are best, or use red onions or shallots)

1/2 teaspoon saffron threads

2 tablespoons olive oil

1 teaspoon each ground ginger, sweet paprika, and cinnamon

2 tablespoons honey

2 tablespoons lemon juice, salt

1 Cut the root end from the onions and pull off the skin. Put the saffron threads into 3/4 cup lukewarm water and leave to soak for a short while until the water turns yellow.

2 Heat the oil in a saucepan. Add the onions and fry for a few minutes over a medium heat until they are lightly browned. Stir from time to time so they don't burn. Sprinkle in the ground ginger, paprika, and cinnamon, then drizzle in the honey. Fry for a few minutes more, then pour in the saffron water and stir to combine.

3 Turn the heat to very low, and cover the pan with a lid. Leave the onions to braise for about 20 minutes, or until they are nicely softened. Check occasionally that there's sufficient water in the pan. If there isn't, just add a little more. Season the onions to taste with lemon juice and salt and leave to cool.

Time you need: 35 minutes
Goes well with: a starter with yogurt and a salad, plus flatbread
Calories per portion: 105

Variation:

Onions with tamarind
Soak 1 tablespoon tamarind (available in good Asian foodstores—if necessary, use tamarind paste instead, but if you do, do not soak this in water) in 3/4 cup lukewarm

water for about 15 minutes, then knead and push through a strainer.Clean the onions as described above and fry in oil. Sprinkle over 1 tablespoon sugar and leave to dissolve. Pour in the tamarind water (or add the paste), season with salt and braise as above. Before serving, sprinkle with freshly chopped cilantro. These onions taste good cold, perhaps even better than hot.

Olives with chermoula
Spicy and good with everything

Serves 4 as a nibble:

2 scallions

2 garlic cloves

1/2 bunch parsley

1/4 bunch cilantro

3 teaspoons ground cumin

3 teaspoons sweet paprika

1 tablespoon lemon juice

4 tablespoons olive oil

salt, ground pepper

1 1/2 cups green olives

1 Cut the root end off the scallions, wash the onions, peel the garlic. Chop all very finely. Wash the herbs and shake them dry. Pull off the leaves and chop very finely.

2 Combine everything with the cumin, paprika, lemon juice, and olive oil, season to taste with a little salt and pepper.

3 Drain the olives if they were pickled in brine. It's best to put them into a strainer and wash them under plenty of cold running water, then drain. Combine them with the chermoula and leave for at least 2 hours (or overnight) to marinate.

Time you need: 15 minutes
(+ 2 hours marinating)
Goes well with: all other appetizers
Calories per portion: 195

Variation:

Marinated feta
1 red chili, 2 garlic cloves, 4 scallions, and 1 bunch parsley—wash everything and trim or peel, then chop very finely. Combine with 5–6 tablespoons olive oil—don't add any salt. Chop about 8 ounces feta into small dice and combine with the marinade. Cover and leave to marinate overnight.

Orange salad with dates

A sweet salad, great with savory food

Serves 4:

4 large, juicy oranges

8 fresh, fleshy dates

1/2 bunch mint

4 tablespoons orange flower water

1 teaspoon sumac

salt

2 teaspoons lemon juice

1/2 teaspoon cinnamon

2 tablespoons olive oil

1/4 cup chopped almonds

1 Cut off a slice from the oranges on both the stem and the opposite ends. Stand the oranges on one of the cut surfaces, then remove all the skin together with the white pith. Slice the oranges crosswise. Catch the juice that escapes while you are cutting. Remove the pits.

2 Remove the pit from the dates and cut the flesh into thin strips. Wash the mint and shake it dry. Pull off the leaves, tear larger ones into smaller pieces.

3 Combine the retained orange juice with the orange flower water, sumac, salt, and lemon juice. Put the oranges onto serving plates, drizzle the sauce over the top, then dust with the cinnamon. Sprinkle the date strips on top.

4 Heat the olive oil in a frying pan. Over a medium heat, fry the almonds in the oil for a few minutes until they are lightly browned, stirring all the time. Season with salt and distribute them over the oranges. Sprinkle with the mint and serve.

Time you need: 20 minutes
Goes well with: chicken or lamb, or the salad can be served as an appetizer.
Calories per portion: 205

1 Dry-roast the cilantro seeds in a small skillet for about 1–2 minutes, or until they start to release a scent. Remove and crush with pestle and mortar.

2 Finely chop the olives. Peel and chop the garlic. Wash the chili, remove the stem end and the seeds, then finely chop the pod.

3 Put the olives, garlic, and chili into an electric blender together with the lemon juice, olive oil, and 2 tablespoons water, and purée until smooth. Stir in the cilantro.

4 Scrape the seeds out of the melon with a spoon. Cut the flesh away from the skin, then chop into dice of about 1/3 inch. Cut the feta into smaller dice too. Combine both on a platter and spoon over the olive sauce. Wash the parsley and shake it dry. Pull off the leaves, chop, and sprinkle them over the melon and cheese.

Time you need: 20 minutes
Goes well with: flatbread,
preferably warm
Calories per portion: 240

Variation:

Orange and tomato salad with olives

Peel and slice 2 juicy oranges, then quarter the slices. Wash 4 tomatoes and cut them into eighths, removing the stem ends. Trim 1 bunch scallions and wash them or peel 2 red onions, then cut into rings or strips. Stir together 2 tablespoons lemon juice, salt, 2 teaspoons sweet paprika, and 1/2 teaspoon ground cumin. Mix in 4 tablespoons olive oil. Combine salad ingredients with the dressing, place a few olives on top, and serve.

Melon and feta with olive sauce

Fruit and cheese—as a side dish or an entrée

Serves 4:

1 1/2 teaspoons cilantro seeds

1 cup pitted green olives

3 garlic cloves

1/2 red chili

2 teaspoons lemon juice

4 tablespoons olive oil

1/2 honeydew melon

5 ounces feta cheese

a few stalks of parsley

1 Separate the lettuce leaves, wash them, and shake them dry. Tear the leaves into smaller pieces. Wash and shake dry the mint, and pull off the leaves. Cut off the root ends of the scallions, wash, and cut into thin rings including all crisp green parts. Combine with the lettuce in a bowl.

2 Finely grate the pistachio kernels (use a nut grinder or an electric blender). Dry-roast in a frying pan over a medium heat, until they release a scent. Make sure they do not burn. Wash the orange under hot water and finely grate the zest and squeeze the juice from one half.

3 Stir together the orange zest and juice, lemon juice, pistachios, and olive oil until you have a creamy sauce, then season with salt, pepper, and cumin to taste. Stir into the salad ingredients in the bowl.

Time you need: 20 minutes
Goes well with: flatbread or
roast lamb
Calories per portion: 210

Variation:

Salad with barberry dressing

Soak 1 tablespoon dried barberries for about 1 hour in 1/4 cup lukewarm water. Combine with about 4 tablespoons olive oil, salt, and pepper. Prepare the salad as described above. A few pieces of cucumber would also go well with it. Stir in the barberry dressing, check the seasoning, and serve.

Salad with pistachio dressing

You could easily get addicted to this!

Serves 4:

1 crunchy lettuce (e.g Romaine or use a mixture of various crunchy salad leaves)

1 small bunch mint

1 bunch scallions

1/3 cup shelled pistachio nuts

1 organic orange

2 tablespoons lemon juice

5 tablespoons olive oil

salt, freshly ground pepper

1 pinch ground cumin

Beets and yogurt

Looks good and tastes good too

Serves 4:

1 pound cooked beets (or canned beets)

1 bunch mint

4 garlic cloves

1 1/3 cups yogurt

3 tablespoons lemon juice

1 teaspoon ground cilantro seeds

salt, ground pepper

1 Cut the beets into very small dice. Beware: Use an old cutting board (perhaps even a plastic one) when you are cutting them because beets stain badly and it is hard to get the cutting surface clean again.

2 Wash the mint and shake it dry. Pull off the leaves and finely chop them. Peel and finely chop the garlic. Combine both with the yogurt and the beets. Season to taste with lemon juice, cilantro, salt, and pepper.

Time you need: 15 minutes
Goes well with: flatbread
Calories per portion: 85

Tip:

Ready-cooked beets save us a lot of trouble. Unfortunately they are usually fairly soft, although this is OK in this yogurt recipe. If you wish to cook them yourself, brush the fresh beets under running cold water. Then place in a saucepan, almost cover with water, cover with a lid, and heat. Cook the beets over a medium heat for 40–60 minutes depending on their size. To check whether they are done, insert the tip of a knife. If the knife slips in easily, they are done. Drain and refresh under cold running water. Leave to cool, then peel, and dice.

Cucumber salad with pomegranate

Looks impressive

Serves 4:

1 large pomegranate

1 cucumber

1 red or mild white onion

1/2 bunch mint (Moroccan Nana mint, if available)

3 tablespoons lemon juice

salt, freshly ground white pepper

1 Halve the pomegranate crosswise. Break the pomegranate into pieces with your hands above a bowl to catch the juice. Separate out the red seeds with your fingers, removing all the white pith because it is bitter. Put the seeds into the bowl.

2 Peel the cucumber and halve it lengthwise. Scrape out the seeds with a spoon. Cut the halves in half again, lengthwise, then cut them into thin slices crosswise. Peel and quarter the onion, and cut it into fine strips.

3 Wash the mint and shake it dry. Pull off and finely chop the leaves. Put into the bowl with the pomegranate seeds, and add the cucumber. Stir in lemon juice, salt, and pepper and leave the salad to marinate for about 1 hour.

Time you need: 25 minutes
(+ 1 hour marinating)
Goes well with: Oriental fried chicken (page 115) or Rice and eggplant bake (page 102)
Calories per portion: 40

Or try this:

If you prefer your salad a little more creamy, stir 2–3 tablespoons yogurt or a little oil into the salad dressing.

Turkish country salad
Quick and easy

Serves 4:

1 pound ripe firm tomatoes

1 cucumber

2 red or white sweet onions

4 pickled banana peppers
(medium hot or mild)

7 ounces feta cheese

2 garlic cloves

1/4 bunch each mint and parsley

4 tablespoons lemon juice

salt, freshly ground white pepper

6 tablespoons olive oil

2 tablespoons black olives

lemon wedges to garnish

1 Wash the tomatoes, cut off the stem ends. Peel the cucumber, or wash, cut in half lengthwise, and scrape out the seeds. Cut tomatoes and cucumber into 1/3 inch dice. Peel and quarter the onions, cut into strips.

2 Cut the banana pepper into medium-thin rings. Roughly grate or crumble the feta cheese. Peel and finely chop or crush the

garlic. Thoroughly wash the mint and the parsley and shake them dry. Pull off the leaves and finely chop them.

3 Stir well to combine the lemon juice with the salt, pepper, and garlic, then gradually beat in the olive oil. Transfer the tomatoes, cucumber, onions, banana pepper, feta, and herbs into a bowl and loosely toss together. Fold in the salad dressing. Don't stir too vigorously because this will make the cheese crumble too much. Place the olives on top of the salad and garnish with lemon wedges.

Time you need: 15 minutes
Goes well with: flatbread
Calories per portion: 385

Variation:

Fiery tomato salad
Wash and very finely chop 1 pound tomatoes, removing the stem ends. Wash, shake dry, and finely chop 1 bunch cilantro. Wash 2 red chilis, remove the stems, finely chop with the seeds. Trim and wash 1 bunch scallions, then finely chop all the crisp parts. Combine the tomatoes with the cilantro, chilis, scallions, and 2–3 tablespoon olive oil and stir well. Season with 1 tablespoon lemon juice, salt, pepper, and 1 teaspoon sugar. Chill until serving. This salad tastes great with kebabs, Turkish pizza, or broiled lamb chops. Or just pile it on some bread.

Roast tomato salad
Sweet, hot, delicious

Serves 4:

1 3/4 pounds tomatoes

5 tablespoons olive oil

2 tablespoons each of honey and lemon juice

1/2 teaspoon harissa (page 95)

salt, freshly ground black pepper

1/2 teaspoon ground ginger

2 tablespoons chopped almonds

1 Preheat oven to 300 °F (convection oven 250 °F without preheating). Wash tomatoes and halve crosswise. Place cut surface up, in a roasting pan, drizzle with 4 tablespoons oil. Bake (center) for about 30 minutes.

2 Leave tomatoes to cool. Spoon flesh out of the skins and chop. Cook juices with the honey for about 5 minutes to reduce. Season with lemon juice and harissa, salt, pepper, and ginger. Stir into the tomatoes. Roast almonds in the remaining oil, sprinkle over.

Time you need: 15 minutes
(+ 30 minutes baking)
Goes well with: flatbread
Calories per portion: 175

Carrot salad with honey dressing

Easy on the budget

Serves 4:

1 pound carrots (similar in

thickness if possible)

1 onion

4 garlic cloves

1 red chili

4 tablespoons olive oil

salt

1/2 organic orange

1/4 bunch each cilantro and parsley

3 tablespoons lemon juice

1 tablespoon runny honey

1 teaspoon sweet paprika

1 Peel the carrots and cut into 1/4 inch slices. Peel and quarter the onion. Cut the quarters into strips, also about 1/4 inch thick. Peel and thinly slice the garlic. Wash the chili and slit open lengthwise. Cut off the stem end and remove the seeds and the white membranes. Cut chili halves into thin strips. Immediately and thoroughly wash your hands so that not too much of the heat remains on them. It's still there, though, so make sure you don't rub your eyes for a while!

2 In a saucepan, heat 2 tablespoons olive oil, add the carrot with the onion, garlic, and chili strips. Fry briefly, stirring, then add 1/4 cup water and season with salt. Cover with the lid, turn the heat to medium, and sauté the carrots for 5–7 minutes. They should still have some bite and not be completely soft. Transfer to a bowl and leave to cool.

3 Meanwhile brush the orange under hot water, then thinly pare off the zest, leaving all the bitter white pith behind, then cut the zest into thin strips. Squeeze the juice from the orange. Wash the herbs and shake them dry. Pull off and finely chop the leaves.

4 Put the orange juice into a little bowl together with the lemon juice, the remaining olive oil, and the honey. Stir until the honey has completely dissolved (this is easiest with a whisk, but you can also use a fork). Season the salad dressing with salt and paprika, then stir it into the carrots. If you have the time, leave the salad for about 1 hour before serving so the flavors can mingle properly. But if you can't bear to wait, just get stuck in right away.

Time you need: 25 minutes
(+ 1 hour marinating)
Goes well with: all other appetizers,
or in summer with grilled meat or fish
Calories per portion: 150

 Basic Tip
Make sure you buy organic
oranges whose skin has not
been treated. If you can't
find any, give them an extra
hard scrub under hot water
to remove the wax and any
other treatments.

Or try this:

Instead of the onion use 1 bunch scallions. Trim, then cut them into thin rings. Do not cook them, but combine them raw with the cilantro and parsley, then stir them into the carrot salad.

Variations:

Carrot salad with pomegranate seeds

Prepare the carrots and cook them without the onions, garlic, and chili. Leave to cool. Peel and finely chop or crush 2 garlic cloves. Wash and shake dry and also finely chop 1/2 bunch parsley. Remove the seeds from 1/2 pomegranate. Wash, trim, and dice 1 tomato and 1 stalk celery. Combine everything. Make a salad dressing from 4 tablespoons lemon juice and 4 tablespoons olive oil, season with salt and pepper, then stir into the salad.

Carrot salad with oranges

Peel 1 pound carrots, but instead of cooking them, finely grate them raw. Thickly cut the zest from 2 oranges along with the white pith. Chop the orange flesh into small dice. Wash, shake dry, and finely chop 1/2 bunch parsley. Combine the juice of 1 orange with 4 tablespoons lemon juice, 2 tablespoons orange flower water, and 2 tablespoons olive oil. Stir in salt, pepper, and 1 teaspoon honey. Combine with the carrots, chopped oranges, and parsley, and chill in the fridge for at least 1 hour. Before serving, finely dust with cinnamon.

Green bean salad with mint
Cold string beans for a change

Serves 4

1 pound young string beans, salt

1 bunch scallions

1 bunch mint, 2 tomatoes

2 garlic cloves

4 tablespoons lemon juice

1/2 teaspoon hot paprika

freshly ground black pepper

4 tablespoons olive oil

lemon wedges to garnish

1 Wash and top and tail the string beans. Put 2 pints water into a large saucepan and bring to a boil. Add plenty of salt, then add the string beans, cover, and simmer over a medium heat for 8–12 minutes until they are still firm. To check, fish one out from time to time and bite into it.

2 When they are done, drain the beans into a colander and refresh with plenty of cold running water. Transfer the beans to a bowl and leave to cool.

3 You have enough time now to prepare the remaining ingredients. Cut the root ends and any wilting parts of the green stems off the scallions. Wash the onions and cut into thin rings. Wash the mint and shake it dry. Pull off the leaves and cut them into thin strips. Wash the tomatoes, cut them into small dice, removing the stem ends. Peel and finely chop the garlic cloves.

4 For the dressing, combine the lemon juice with the paprika, salt, and pepper and stir well to mix. With a fork, beat in the olive oil, a little at a time. Add the dressing together with the scallions, tomatoes, garlic, and mint to the beans in the bowl. Mix well and check for seasoning. If there is sufficient salt and pepper, garnish the salad with the lemon wedges and serve.

Time you need: 30 minutes
Goes well with: flatbread
Calories per portion: 140

Quick version:
Instead of string beans, use canned white haricot beans. Replace the scallions with 1–2 red onions. Peel and halve the onions, then cut them into strips. Combine with the white haricot beans and the remaining ingredients and mix well.

Golden cauliflower salad
Sunshine in a bowl

Serves 4:

1 smallish cauliflower (about 1 1/2 pounds)

salt

1/2 tablespoon ground turmeric

1/2 bunch each parsley, mint, and cilantro

1 tablespoon sesame paste (tahini)

2 tablespoons yogurt

3–4 tablespoons lemon juice

1 teaspoon sweet paprika

2 tablespoons olive oil

4 tablespoons pine nuts or sunflower seeds

1 Wash and trim cauliflower. Separate into small florets. Dice the stems. Pour 4 pints water into a large saucepan, add salt and turmeric, and bring to a boil. Add florets and stems, cover, and cook over a medium heat for 5–8 minutes until firm. Don't let the cauliflower get too soft.

2 Drain the cauliflower in a colander, and quickly refresh under cold water. Leave cauliflower to cool.

3 In the meantime, wash the herbs and shake them dry. Pull off and finely chop the leaves. To make the dressing, combine the sesame paste with the yogurt and the lemon juice using a whisk. Season with salt and paprika to taste.

4 Heat the oil in a skillet. Add the pine nuts or sunflower seeds and fry until they are golden brown, stirring all the time. Fold the herbs into the cauliflower and transfer to a serving platter. Drizzle the sauce over the top and sprinkle with the pine nuts or seeds.

Time you need: 30 minutes
Goes well with: flatbread and
a few olives
Calories per portion: 175

Variation:

Red cauliflower salad
Replace half the cooking water with beet juice, or color it with food coloring. Prepare the salad as described above.

Hot vegetable salad
Colorful and tasty

Serves 4:

1 large eggplant (about 1 pound)

1 large red and 1 large green bell pepper

2 medium onions

4 garlic cloves

1 bunch parsley

4 tablespoons olive oil

2 teaspoons sugar

1/2 tablespoon sweet paprika

6 tablespoons lemon juice

1 teaspoon ground cumin

salt, freshly ground black pepper

1 teaspoon sumac

1 Preheat the oven to 450 °F (heat convection oven to 400 °F).

2 Wash the eggplant and halve it length-wise. Wash the bell peppers and also halve them lengthwise. Remove the stems, seeds, and white membranes. Line a roasting pan with parchment paper or foil and place the vegetable halves, skin side up, on the tray. Roast the vegetables in the center of the

oven for about 20 minutes until the skin of the bell peppers has turned dark and starts to blister.

3 Remove the vegetables from the oven and leave to cool a little. Skin the peppers and dice the flesh. Remove the eggplant flesh from the skins with a spoon and also dice it.

4 Peel and finely chop the onions and the garlic. Wash the parsley and shake it dry. Pull off the leaves and finely chop them.

5 Heat the olive oil in a skillet, add the onions and the garlic, and fry over a medium heat for 3–4 minutes, stirring. Sprinkle in the sugar and continue frying until the onions are a golden yellow. Add the paprika and stir well to combine.

6 Put the pepper and eggplant dice into the pan together with half the parsley, stir to combine, and heat through. Add the lemon juice and season the vegetables with cumin, salt, and pepper. Transfer to a serving dish. Sprinkle with the remaining parsley and the sumac. Serve the salad hot.

Time you need: 45 minutes
Goes well with: flatbread and
yogurt as a cold appetizer.
Calories per portion: 155

Bread salad
Known as *fattoush* in Syria

Serves 4 as a main course:

1 flatbread

3 tomatoes

1 green bell pepper

1 small cucumber

1 handful of mixed lettuce leaves (e.g. Romaine, iceberg)

1 bunch parsley

1/4 bunch mint

2 garlic cloves

1 bunch scallions

6 tablespoons lemon juice

6 tablespoons olive oil

1 teaspoon sumac

salt, freshly ground black pepper

1 Preheat the oven to 450 °F (preheat convection oven now to 400 °F) or preheat broiler to high. Slice open the flatbread and place with the cut surface up directly on a rack. Bake in the oven (center) for a few minutes until nice and crisp. Take out and leave to cool, then break into small pieces.

2 Wash the vegetables. Remove the stem ends from the tomatoes. Remove the stems, seeds, and membranes from the bell peppers. Cut tomatoes, bell peppers, and cucumber into small dice. Wash the lettuce leaves and shake them dry, then tear into smaller pieces. Wash herbs and shake them dry. Pull off the leaves and finely chop them.

3 Peel and finely chop the garlic. Cut the root ends off the scallions and remove any limp or dried out bits. Cut into thin rings.

4 Stir lemon juice with the olive oil, sumac, salt, and pepper to combine. Pour the dressing over the prepared ingredients, stir together and leave to marinate for about 30 minutes. Stir again, check the seasoning and adjust if needed; serve immediately.

Time you need: 20 minutes
(+ 30 minutes marinating)
Goes well with: a few olives,
but no extra flatbread required!
Calories per portion: 540

Garbanzo salad
Leaves you happy and satisfied

Serves 4:

1 can garbanzos (14 ounces approx.)

1 red onion

1 small red and 1 small green bell pepper

1 stalk celery, 3 tomatoes

1/2 bunch parsley

2 tablespoons pitted green olives

3 garlic cloves

4 tablespoons sesame paste (tahini)

5 tablespoons yogurt

3 tablespoons lemon juice

salt, freshly ground black pepper

1 teaspoon sweet paprika

2 tablespoons red wine vinegar

4 tablespoons olive oil

4 ounces feta cheese

1 Drain the garbanzos in a colander and wash under cold water. Drain again. Peel and quarter the onion, then cut it into thin strips. Wash the vegetables. Halve the bell peppers, remove stems, seeds, and membranes. Cut off the ends of the celery. Remove any

strings. Cut the stem ends off the tomatoes. Cut peppers and tomatoes into small dice, and the celery into thin slices.

2 Wash the parsley and shake it dry. Pull off the leaves and finely chop them. Slice the olives. Peel and finely chop the garlic.

3 Using a hand-held blender or a food processor, mix together the garlic, the sesame paste, yogurt, 1 tablespoon water, and lemon juice. Season with salt, pepper, and paprika. Stir the vinegar into the oil and season with salt and pepper.

4 Combine the garbanzos with the onion, bell peppers, tomatoes, celery, parsley, and olives, then stir in the vinegar and oil dressing. Transfer the salad to small serving plates or bowls. Crumble the cheese into small pieces and distribute around the edge of each serving. Spoon a bit of sesame sauce into the center of each dish. That's it!

Time you need: 25 minutes
Goes well with: flatbread
Calories per portion: 345

Or try this:
Instead of garbanzos, use canned white haricot beans. Replace the celery with a cucumber, and instead of the cheese use hard-boiled eggs. Shell and quarter these and arrange them around the salad.

Tabouleh
Nice and green

Serves 4:

1 cup fine bulgur wheat (available from health food stores and well-stocked supermarkets) or couscous

2–3 bunches parsley (the exact amount depends on the size of the bunch, but there should be plenty)

1/2 bunch mint

3 tomatoes

4 scallions

1 green chili (for those who like it hot, but you can leave it out if you prefer)

5 tablespoons lemon juice

5 tablespoons olive oil

salt, freshly ground black pepper

1 Pour the bulgur wheat or couscous into a bowl. Add sufficient lukewarm water to just cover the grains, then leave them to soak for 20 minutes.

2 In the meantime, wash the herbs and shake them dry. Pull off the leaves and chop them very finely. Remove stem ends from the tomatoes, pour boiling water over them, then

skin the tomatoes, and refresh under cold water. Halve them, and cut out the seeds. Chop the tomato flesh into small dice. Cut the root ends off the scallions. Wash the white parts and chop them very finely. Wash the chili and slit it open lengthwise. Remove the stem and the seeds. Very finely chop the chili (wash your hands after that!).

3 Drain the bulgur wheat or couscous through a fine-meshed strainer. Combine the lemon juice with the oil, salt, and pepper, then stir the dressing into the grains. Add the vegetables, chili, and herbs and stir everything well together. Check and adjust the seasoning if necessary. Serve.

Time you need: 35 minutes
Goes well with: fresh salad leaves to serve
Calories per portion: 295

Or try this:
Add some cucumber dice to the salad. Season the salad additionally with some ground cumin and hot paprika.

Street

Ah, the smell of falafels and kababs

Fare

Let's get out, leave the house, go out through the large gate.
We'll leave our tranquil inner courtyard where a light wind gently
strokes the curtains.

We'll venture into the noisy alleyways, where merchants sing
the praise of their wares, and cups of mokka invite us to linger.
A sip, a sigh, and we drift along, always following the crowd.

A smell of roast lamb wafts through the streets, followed by freshly
baked flatbread, kebabs, and falafel. And all of that laced with
plenty of garlic! This is the Orient in the heat of noon. So let's
have a bite to eat. And let us sit down to do so. For even a humble
doner kebab commands repose and respect.

What the Orient drinks

Mokka with cardamom

Oh, how delightful is a cup of Arabica when it is prepared in the way of the Orient—nice and sweet, with its grounds and a hint of cardamom. Whether it's a Turkish "kahve" or an Arabic "mokka"—coffee, water, and (usually) sugar are always put on the fire together, and then, after a bit of magical brewing, the mixture is transferred into small cups, beakers, or glasses, foaming and aromatic. We'll combine the traditions and take the simpler way of preparing it from the "kahve" (one less step) and the spice (cardamom) from the "mokka." But one thing is a must: the "cezve," as the little copper pot with the long handle is called in Turkish. The coffee foams best in this. That and of course the very finely ground coffee which we can buy at the deli around the corner.

To make 2 cups, fill the pot with 1/2 cup water, then slowly stir in 2 teaspoons sugar, 2 heaped tablespoons Turkish coffee and 2 cardamom pods without letting the spoon drop—so goes the ritual. Onto the fire or the stove with it, continuing to stir from outside to the center for the best foam. Just before it reaches boiling point, a generous glug of the coffee is poured into each cup to warm it through. Now stir it again on the fire until the liquid starts to simmer. Then pour the coffee with plenty of foam into the cups and leave to stand so the grounds can settle. And enjoy!

From the first apple...

...to the Last Supper

It all began with the apple, and it ended with the Last Supper. If you like, you can find references to all sorts of foods in the Bible. After all, this is a text from the Orient where people know as much about pleasure as about applying wisdom to everyday life. And that can best be done over a meal. Whether it is the prodigal son returning home or three angels appearing to Abraham—on each occasion a young animal was slaughtered to stress the importance of the event. Meat was eaten only on special and festive days, and the meat of young lambs and calves was especially valuable.

Joseph was sold to traders by his brother for "saddle bags filled with spices;" Jacob bought the right to his elder brother's inheritance for a bowl of lentil soup; Jesus fed the 5,000 with five loaves and two fish—the stories in the Bible tell us what people used to eat in biblical days: bread, fish, and pulses for ordinary folk, seasoned with the biblical "bitter herbs" such as dill, cilantro, marjoram, parsley, thyme. Meat and spices were reserved for the rich.

One story still poses a puzzle for us today: When, after their flight from Egypt, the hungry Israelites dreamed of steaming pots of meat and fish and garlic and onions, God made flocks of quails drop out of the sky—and today these birds are still considered a luxury in the Orient. But what were the grains that were strewn over the ground every day thereafter and that fed the people until they arrived in the Promised Land? Moses described them as "white cilantro seeds" with a "flavor of honeybuns" and he called them "manna." What exactly they were, we still don't know today.

On haggling

Ingenious Genie!

I bought a leather belt for our friend back home. And I didn't even have to haggle—the price I was given seemed good and fair to me. But, after that, just one stall along, no one was willing to sell me anything. Why?

Tse, tse*, my friend— you must (!) always (!!) haggle, however much you like the price you are told. The trader will feel insulted if you do not try to acquire his good wares by haggling. And the news will spread faster than the wind can whistle. So let us practice straight away.

Once you've discovered something you wish to buy, casually inquire about the price and decide for yourself what you would really want to spend on it. Once you have been given a price, critically examine the item, praise it, and say what you think it is worth—naming a price lower than you had decided you'd be willing to pay and very much lower than what the trader had asked for. Now he will tell you that business has been bad and that he has many mouths to feed. Listen and wait to be given a new price. Then the next step is up to you again.

If you do not meet each other's prices, put the item down and ask if he has anything better or whether he can add something else for the same price. Always negotiate well, fairly, and peacefully. If it doesn't seem to work, he may just not feel like selling anything at the moment. If so, continue to the next stall with a friendly regret— and return the following day.

*What does this mean? Read the answer on page 145.

Home-made Oriental Basics

Yogurt

Yogurt is the milk of the Orient—and there is a very simple reason for that: In the scorching heat of the day, the fresh milk of the cow, goat, or sheep (occasionally also of the mare or the buffalo) hardly had sufficient time to reach the table before beginning to turn sour. This is why people made the milk into a soured substance such as yogurt straight away, making sure it didn't go "off." And we can do the same at home, very easily and without a machine:

Quickly bring to a boil 1 quart fresh full-fat milk, then leave to cool down to 100 °F in a warm place. Combine this with 1 carton fresh plain yogurt at room temperature, cover and leave to stand in a warm place (again around 100 °F) for at least 8 hours. If you like it sour, leave for another 8 hours maximum. Now put the yogurt into the fridge to chill for 1–2 days, and it'll be really excellent.

What does it mean...

...Doner Kebab?

In the Turkish part of Vienna, an absent-minded Viennese psychiatrist is supposed to have said to his wife that this guy Doner must be a great businessman— having opened so many eating establishments! And perhaps the first part of the name does sound somewhat familiar—Doner Kebab—the food that has turned it into one of the top favorite street foods the world over. It's a different story in its hometown, Istanbul: Here, meat from the revolving spit is just one popular snack among very many. And it looks different too: Slices of lamb or mutton, alternated with ground meat, are placed around the spit and grilled over charcoal, then pushed onto a plate—just as it was once supposedly presented to a Sultan—he was to have been served an entire roast lamb without being subjected to the ignominy of biting on a bone. Only the export version transformed the lamb into veal, turkey, or beef, and added plenty of ground meat (but not more than 60 percent) as well as the pita pocket. Here as there, "kebab" means "roasted meat" and "doner" means "turning" or the spit it rotates on. "Doner Kebab" therefore simply translates as "spit-roasted meat." By the way, someone once tried to trademark the name and cash in handsomely. Perhaps the Viennese psychiatrist wasn't quite so absent-minded after all?

Pita bread
Accompanies almost every meal

Makes 2 breads:

3 1/3 cups flour + flour for the work surface

1 heaped teaspoon salt

1 ounce cake yeast

2 teaspoons sugar

3 tablespoons canola oil + oil for handling

1 egg

4 tablespoon sesame seeds

1 tablespoon black cumin seeds

1 In a bowl, mix the flour with the salt. Crumble the yeast into a cup, add 1 teaspoon sugar and 1 1/2 cups lukewarm water and stir well to combine.

2 Add the yeast mixture and 2 tablespoons oil to the flour, then knead with the kneading hooks of a hand-held blender. The dough should still be soft enough to stick to your fingers, so don't even start to knead it with your hands!

3 Cover the dough with a clean cloth and leave to rest for about 40 minutes. Now turn it out onto a well-floured working surface and knead vigorously with your hands—for at least 5 minutes. Return the dough to the bowl, cover it again, and leave it to rise for a further 40 minutes.

4 Preheat the oven to 480 °F (also preheat convections ovens now to 425 °F). Line two cookie sheets with parchment paper. Knead the dough again, then divide it into two halves. Shape each half into a flat patty about 10 inches in diameter. Place them on the cookie sheets.

5 Stir together the egg, the remaining sugar, and the remaining oil. Moisten your fingertips with a little oil, and press a diamond shape into each flat bread. Brush the breads with the egg-oil-mixture. Combine the sesame and the cumin and sprinkle the breads with the spice mixture.

6 Bake the breads, one after the other, in the oven (center) for 12–15 minutes. After half the baking time, sprinkle a little cold water onto the bottom of the oven and immediately close the oven door again. Place the breads on a rack to cool.

Time you need: 30 minutes
(+ just under 2 hours resting and baking)
Goes well with: all appetizers, but also with meat, fish, and vegetable dishes
Calories per bread: 1265

Variations:

Pitas with sumac
Prepare the dough as described above and leave to rest. Combine 1 tablespoon dried thyme with 1 tablespoon sumac, 1 tablespoon sesame seeds, salt, coarsely ground pepper, and 1/2 teaspoon sugar. Shape the breads and bake for 5 minutes. Brush with water, sprinkle with the spice mixture, and bake until done.

Wholewheat pittas
Replace half the flour with wholewheat flour or perhaps barley flour for a change. Add a little more water when kneading because wholewheat flour is more absorbent. Shape and bake as before.

Small puffed breads
Use 1 1/2 ounces cake yeast and replace about 1 cup of the flour with wholewheat flour. Prepare the dough as described. Shape it into 6–7 smaller breads and place them on the cookie sheets to rise for a further 15 minutes, then bake for about 10 minutes. These breads will puff up even more than the ordinary pitas—ideal for filling.

Pita bread with butter
Melt 1/2 stick butter, but do not let it brown. Dissolve 1 ounce cake yeast together with 1 teaspoon sugar in 3/4 cup water, add to 3 1/2 cups flour together with 1 egg and combine well. Add the butter and 1 1/2 teaspoons salt, briefly knead everything. Halve and shape into breads. Place onto parchment paper, cover, and leave to rest for about 1 hour. Brush with 1 egg yolk and bake for about 20 minutes at 390 °F (convection oven 350 °F).

Sesame rings
Make a dough from 3 1/2 cups flour, salt, 2/3 ounce cake yeast and about 1 cup lukewarm water, leave to rise. Divide into 8 portions, shape each into long rolls, then into rings. Brush with 1 beaten egg, sprinkle with sesame seeds, and leave to rise for another 15 minutes. Bake rings for about 20 minutes at 390 °F (convection oven 350 °F).

Sweet bread rolls
Great for breakfast: Dissolve 1 1/2 ounces cake yeast in 3/4 cup lukewarm milk with 1 teaspoon sugar, briefly leave to stand. Quickly toast 1 tablespoon anise seeds in a frying pan, then crush them with pestle and mortar. Add 1/4 cup sugar to 3 1/2 cups flour. Combine the yeast mixture with 1/2 stick melted butter and 5 tablespoons canola oil, 1 egg, and 5 tablespoons orange flower water. Knead to a smooth dough. Place in a bowl, cover, leave to rise for about 40 minutes. Knead again, shape into 10 rolls. Place on a cookie sheet lined with parchment paper. Cover and leave to rise for a further 30 minutes. Brush with 1 beaten egg yolk, sprinkle with sesame seeds, and bake for 15 minutes at 390 °F (convection oven 350 °F).

Pitas from the skillet
Great for filling

Makes 12 breads:

3 1/2 cups flour + flour for the work surface

1 ounce cake yeast

1 teaspoon sugar

1 teaspoon salt

1 Put the flour into a bowl. Crumble the yeast, and stir in 1 cup lukewarm water and the sugar. Add to the flour together with the salt and knead vigorously. Cover and leave to rise for 1 hour.

2 On a floured working surface, vigorously knead the dough with your hands, then divide into 12 portions. Roll each one out to make a thin bread.

3 Heat a nonstick skillet. Cook the breads, one at a time, for 1–2 minutes on each side over a high heat. Wrap the fried breads in a clean cloth to keep them warm and soft.

Time you need: 1 hour
(+ 1 hour resting)
Goes well with: everything that you may wish to wrap in thin pitas: for example meat kebabs.
Calories per bread: 155

Turkish pizza with chopped meat
Move aside, Italy!

Serves 4:

For the dough:

1/3 ounce cake yeast

1/2 teaspoon sugar

3 cups flour + flour for the work surface

1 teaspoon salt, 1 tablespoon oil

For the topping:

2 onions, 2 garlic cloves

2 tablespoons olive oil

1 pound shoulder of lamb or veal scallopini

2 tomatoes, 1 bunch parsley

2 teaspoons tomato paste

2 teaspoons sweet paprika

1 tablespoon sumac

salt, freshly ground pepper

1 To make the dough, crumble the yeast in a small bowl, stir in the sugar and 1 cup lukewarm water. Add to the flour with the salt and oil, and knead until you have a smooth dough. Shape into a ball, cover, and leave to rise for about 1 hour.

2 Meanwhile, make the topping: Peel and finely chop onions and garlic. Heat the oil and fry onions and garlic over a medium heat for about 5 minutes, or until half-softened, stirring all the time. Transfer to a bowl.

3 Trim the meat of fat and sinews. Now first cut the meat into small dice, then chop with a large knife until it looks like ground meat. Add to the onions.

4 Preheat the oven to 450 °F (convection oven to 390 °F). Cut the stem ends from the tomatoes. Briefly plunge tomatoes into boiling water, skin, halve, and deseed them. Chop tomatoes into small dice. Wash the parsley and shake dry. Finely chop the leaves. Add tomatoes, parsley, tomato paste, paprika, and sumac to the bowl and mix everything well. Season with salt and pepper.

5 Knead the dough on a floured working surface. Divide it into 8 portions and roll out each portion into a thin circle. Line a cookie sheet with parchment paper. Place the first group of pizzas on the cookie sheet (it should hold 4 pizzas), and spread with the chopped meat filling.

6 Push the pizzas into the oven (center) and throw 1/2 cup cold water into the bottom of the oven. Immediately close the oven door and bake the pizzas for 8–10 minutes. The meat should be well cooked, but the dough

should still be soft enough to roll. Remove them from the oven, roll up each pizza, and eat. Time to bake the rest.

Time you need: 50 minutes
(+ 1 hour 10 minutes resting and baking)
Goes well with: Cover the breads with Fiery tomato salad (page 49) before rolling them
Calories per portion: 550

Variation:

Pizza with feta cheese
Instead of the ground meat, crumble 10 ounces feta cheese and purée together with 1 1/4 cups sheep milk yogurt. Stir in 1 large egg. Spread the pizzas with the mixture, sprinkle with cumin seeds, and bake. Cover with some sliced green chilis, roll up—and enjoy.

Tunesian sandwich
Luxury snack

Serves 4:

3 bell peppers (mixed red and green)

3 tomatoes, 3 garlic cloves

1 teaspoon cilantro seeds

2 tablespoons lemon juice

3 tablespoons olive oil

salt, freshly ground pepper

1 can tuna (6 ounces, if possible in olive oil)

1 tablespoon capers

1 teaspoon harissa (page 95)

4 small pitas

4–8 lettuce leaves

1 Preheat the oven to 480 °F (convection oven to 425 °F). Line a cookie sheet with parchment paper. Wash and halve the bell peppers and the tomatoes. Remove the stems, seeds and white membranes from the peppers. Place peppers and tomatoes onto the cookie sheet, skin side up. Add the unpeeled garlic. Bake in the oven (center) for 20 minutes, or until the peppers blister.

2 Remove the vegetables from the oven and leave to cool a little. Skin the bell peppers (the green ones are more difficult). Skin the tomatoes and with a spoon scrape out some of the seeds. Halve the garlic cloves and spoon the flesh from the skins.

3 Pile peppers, tomatoes, and garlic onto a large chopping board. Finely chop with a large heavy knife. Transfer to a bowl. Grind the cilantro seeds. Stir into the vegetables together with the lemon juice and 2 table-spoons oil. Season with salt and pepper.

4 Drain the tuna and flake with a fork. Combine with the capers, harissa, and the remaining oil, season with salt. Slit the pitas open. Wash the lettuce leaves and shake dry. Cover the bottom halves of the pita with the lettuce. Spread with the pepper and tomato mixture (which is known as *mechouia* and makes a great appetizer on its own too) and the tuna. Cover with the pita tops. That's it.

Time you need: 20 minutes
(+ 20 minutes baking)
Calories per portion: 575

Oriental wrap
Good and filling

Serves 4:

For the dough:

1/3 ounce cake yeast, 1/2 teaspoon sugar

3 cups flour + flour for work surface

1 teaspoon salt, 1 tablespoon oil

For the filling:

3/4 cup fine bulgur wheat

2 tomatoes, 2 garlic cloves

1/2 bunch each parsley and mint

2 tablespoons lemon juice

4 tablespoons olive oil

salt, freshly ground pepper

8 ounces boneless lamb or filet mignon

1 teaspoon ground cumin, 4–8 lettuce leaves

1/2 portion hummus (page 40)

1 Prepare the dough as described for the pizzas and leave to rise.

2 Cover the bulgur wheat with lukewarm water and leave to swell for 30 minutes. Wash and finely dice the tomatoes, cutting off the stem ends. Peel and finely chop the garlic. Wash, shake dry, and finely chop the herbs. Drain the bulgur, combine with the chopped ingredients, and stir in the lemon juice and 2 tablespoons oil. Season.

3 Cut meat into thin strips and combine with the salt, pepper, and cumin. Shape the dough into thin round breads and bake as for the pizza. Wrap in a cloth to keep warm. Wash the lettuce and shake dry .

4 Heat the remaining oil and fry the meat over a high heat for 2–3 minutes. Cover the breads with lettuce, then spread with the bulgur salad, place the meat on top and garnish with hummus. Roll up and enjoy!

Time you need: 30 minutes
(+ 1 hour rising and swelling)
Calories per portion: 845

63

Feta cheese rolls

Also known as cigarette *böreks*

Serves 4 as an appetizer or

to nibble with drinks:

1 pound feta cheese

1/2 bunch each dill and parsley

2 eggs

1 teaspoon hot paprika

freshly ground pepper

6 round leaves yufka or filo pastry

3 cups oil for deep-frying

1 Try a little of the feta cheese. If it tastes very salty, soak it in some cold water for about 15 minutes to make it a little milder. Then remove from the water and mash well with a fork.

2 Wash the dill and the parsley and shake dry. Pinch off the thicker stems, then finely chop the leaves and the remaining stems. Stir herbs and eggs into the cheese, then season with paprika and pepper. You won't need to add any salt—the cheese will still contain plenty of that.

3 Carefully separate the pastry leaves. They are so thin that they will easily tear if you are not careful. Place pairs of the leaves on top of each other and cut these into 16 equal-sized "cake slices."

4 Spread the filling onto the wider side of the cut pastry leaves. Brush the pastry edges with cold water. Now start rolling up the leaves as if rolling a cigarette, firmly pressing the edges together.

5 Heat the oil in a wide saucepan. Check the temperature with a wooden spoon: As soon as many little bubbles form all around it, the oil is hot enough.

6 Place the pastry rolls, a few at a time, into the hot oil and deep-fry for about 3 minutes, or until they are nicely golden brown. Lift them out with a slotted spoon, then place them on paper towels to soak up some of the fat. As soon as all are deep-fried, serve the rolls hot.

Time you need: 1 hour
Goes well with: cucumber yogurt (as on page 43, but leave out raisins and walnuts, and season instead with garlic)
Calories per portion: 595

Briouats with ground meat

Also known as böureks, borekas, or briks

Serves 6 as an appetizer or

4 as an entrée:

1 small onion

4 garlic cloves

2 tablespoons oil

1/2 bunch each parsley and mint

1/2 pound ground lamb or beef

1 teaspoon each sweet paprika, freshly grated nutmeg, and ground cilantro

1 tablespoon lemon juice

salt, freshly ground pepper

2 leaves yufka or 4 leaves filo pastry (use square leaves, if possible) or 4 leaves frozen puff pastry and a little flour

1/2 stick butter

1 Peel and very finely chop the onion and the garlic. Heat the oil in a skillet. Over a medium heat, fry the onion and the garlic for about 10 minutes, until they are softened but not yet browned. Transfer to a bowl.

2 Wash the herbs and shake them dry. Pull off the leaves and very finely chop them. Add herbs and ground meat to the onions. Stir in the paprika, nutmeg, cilantro, and the lemon juice, and season to taste with salt and pepper. Knead everything well so it sticks together.

3 And now it depends on which type of pastry you are using: Carefully separate the yufka pastry leaves. Melt the butter, but do not allow it to brown. Cut the pastry leaves into strips, about 4 inches wide and a good 8 inches long. Brush them with a little butter.

4 Filo pastry: Brush 2 pastry leaves with a little butter, then cover each pair with one unbuttered pastry leaf. Cut the pastry packs into strips as above.

5 Puff pastry: This needs to be defrosted first, but luckily that's quick, and only takes about 15–20 minutes. To do so, separate the pastry leaves and leave them to thaw under a paper towel so they don't dry out too much. Then roll out on a little flour, as thinly as possible, and cut as above.

6 Start imagining now how you are going to turn the strips into triangles. It's just like origami. You start on the left: Spread just under 1 tablespoon of the filling on the first third at the bottom right (see picture 1). Fold the upper left corner down over this to the bottom right. The first triangle is formed

(see picture 2). Now the entire triangle is folded to the right, and then up, and then again to the right. And if there's a tiny bit of pastry still left, just wrap that over the triangle (see picture 3). Done!

7 Preheat the oven to 385 °F (convection oven to 350 °F). Line a cookie sheet with parchment paper. Place the pastry triangles onto the cookie sheet and brush with the remaining butter. Bake the pastry triangles in the oven (center) for about 15 minutes, or until they are nicely browned. Serve them hot or lukewarm for the best flavor.

Time you need: 45 minutes
(+ 15 minutes baking, plus thawing time if using puff pastry)
Goes well with: cucumber yogurt
(as on page 43, possibly without raisins),
Roast tomato salad (page 49), or fiery pepper paste (page 40)
Calories per portion: 260

Or try this:
Brush the pastry edges with egg white—this makes them stick together really well—and then deep-fry the pastry pockets in plenty of hot oil for 3–4 minutes, or until golden brown. Leave to drain on some absorbent paper towels. This method is not so well suited for puff pastry, however.

Variations:

Tuna filling
Peel and finely grate 2 onions. Peel, crush, and add 2 garlic cloves. Wash, shake dry, and chop 1 bunch parsley. Combine everything with 1 can tuna in oil (6 ounces) and season with salt, pepper, and 1/2 teaspoon harissa (page 95).

Chicken filling
Cut 1/2 pound cooked or uncooked chicken into very fine dice. Peel and finely chop 1 onion and 2 garlic cloves, then fry in 1 tablespoon oil for 5 minutes. Stir a pinch of saffron threads in 5 tablespoons lukewarm water, then add. Cook to reduce a little, then stir into the chicken. Wash, shake dry, and chop 1 large bunch cilantro; add to the chicken. Season with salt, pepper, and 1/2 tablespoon sweet paprika. Stir well.

Potato filling
Peel, wash, and dice 2 waxy potatoes. Peel and roughly chop 1 onion. Put both in plenty of salted water and bring to a boil. Cover and simmer until cooked. Drain, mash with a fork and stir in 2 tablespoons olive oil, 1 chopped hard-boiled egg, 1 large bunch chopped parsley, and 1/2 can tuna in olive oil (6 ounces). Season with salt, pepper, and 1 teaspoon ras-el-hanout (page 113).

Doner
from the wok
Turkish food cooked Chinese-style

Serves 4:

For the meat:

1 1/2 pounds leg of lamb (boned), or
filet mignon, or veal scallopini

2 stalks mint

2 garlic cloves

1 onion

1 teaspoon each sweet paprika, ground
cumin, and ground cilantro

4 tablespoons olive oil

salt, freshly ground pepper

For the topping:

1 small cucumber (about 5 ounces)

1 garlic clove

1 cup firm yogurt (if possible, use
sheep milk yogurt)

salt, freshly ground pepper

2 Bermuda onions

2 tomatoes

4–8 lettuce leaves (use more or less
depending on size)

1 sesame bread or

4 small pitas

1 Remove any large pieces of fat and any thick sinews from the meat. Cut the meat into thin strips. Wash the mint and shake dry. Pull off the leaves and finely chop them. Peel the garlic and the onion. Crush the garlic, finely grate the onion, or chop it very finely in a food processor.

2 Combine the spices with the oil, mint, garlic, and onion purée and stir well. Stir in the meat strips, cover and chill in the fridge for at least 4 hours. Take out occasionally and stir everything.

3 To make the topping, wash or peel the cucumber, then halve it lengthwise. Scrape out the seeds with a spoon. Finely grate the cucumber flesh, using a kitchen grater. Peel the garlic cloves, crush them, and add them to the yogurt. Stir in the grated cucumber, then season the yogurt with salt and pepper to taste.

4 Peel the onions, then cut them into thin rings. Wash the tomatoes and cut out the stem ends as a wedge. Thinly slice the tomatoes—this is most easily done using a knife with a serrated edge. Briefly wash the lettuce leaves under cold water, then shake or spin-dry well.

5 Preheat the oven to 480 °F (convection oven also now to 425 °F). Place the wok on top of the stove and heat it to very hot. If you don't have a wok, use a skillet instead. But make sure it's a very large pan, and if possible use a heavy cast-iron one.

6 Put the bread into the oven (center) and allow to warm through. In the meantime, cook the meat strips in two portions in the wok—without any added oil—and stir-fry for 2–3 minutes, stirring all the time. Season them now with salt and pepper. When cooked, place the first portion into the oven with the bread to keep warm.

7 Remove the bread from the oven and quarter it. Diagonally cut open each quarter. Cover the bottom halves with lettuce leaves, tomatoes (salt them lightly), and onion rings. Divide the meat strips on top and spoon the cucumber yogurt over the meat. Cover with the top halves of the breads and enjoy.

Time you need: 35 minutes
(+ 4 hours marinating)
Calories per portion: 915

Or try this:

If you like it hot, season the yogurt with a little harissa (page 95). Olives are also good in the bread (use pitted ones, otherwise eating is no fun). A few mild pickled banana peppers are another tasty addition.

Basic Tip

Everyone talks about it: It's healthy to eat low fat. It's no wonder then that even doner kebab stalls now offer you their low-fat turkey variations. Which of course you can also use to make the Doner in this recipe. But we actually think the classic version with lamb or beef is better. Turkey dries out very easily. Unless it's an organic bird, we don't really care for it anyway.

Falafel
Perfect with peas

Serves 4 as a dip:

1 1/2 cups split peas (green or yellow), fava

beans, or garbanzos—all dried

2 onions

2 garlic cloves

1/2 bunch each parsley and cilantro

1 teaspoon each ground cilantro, ground

cumin, and sweet paprika

2 teaspoons salt

1 teaspoon baking powder

3 cups oil for deep-frying

1 Put the pulses into a bowl, add sufficent water to cover them completely, then leave to soak over night.

2 The following day, peel and roughly chop the onions and the garlic. Wash the herbs and shake them dry. Pull off the leaves. Drain the pulses in a colander and put them into a food processor. Add the onions, garlic, and herbs and purée everything as smoothly as possible. If you have a meat grinder at home or a food mill you could use that instead.

3 Combine the spices with the salt and the

baking powder, then add the mixture to the falafel purée. Stir well to mix and form into about 40 small balls. You can't really roll them into this shape; instead shape the purée between your hands.

4 Heat the oil in a heavy Dutch oven until very hot. Place a wooden spoon in the pan; as soon as many little bubbles form everywhere, the oil is hot enough.

5 Deep-fry the little balls in the oil, a few at a time, for about 4–5 minutes each, or until they look nicely golden brown. Fish them out with a slotted spoon and place them on some paper towels to drain. The falafel are best served hot, but they are also tasty once they've cooled.

Time you need: 40 minutes
(+ soaking over night)
Goes well with: fiery pepper paste (page 40, possibly combined with yogurt), hot tomato salad (page 49), or cucumber salad with pomegranate (page 48)
Calories per portion: 260

Variation:

Vegetable koftas
Peel and dice 1 pound carrots, turnips and/or kohlrabi. Cook the dice in plenty salted water until soft. Drain, the squash until smooth or purée. Grate or purée

2 slices one-day-old bread and lightly toast the crumbs in a dry skillet. Finely chop 2 tablespoons unsalted pistachio nuts. Wash 1/2 bunch each of mint and parsley and shake dry. Pull off the leaves and finely chop them. Peel and crush 2 garlic cloves. Combine everything with 1 teaspoon sweet paprika, 1 egg yolk, and 1/2 cup flour, then season to taste with salt and pepper. Shape into little balls or longish cigars. Deep-fry in plenty of hot olive or sunflower oil for about 4–5 minutes, fish out, and place on paper towels to drain well. Serve with yogurt (flavored with lime zest and garlic, or with cucumber and mint).

Authentic eating:
Falafel are rarely served by themselves, but are usually wrapped in flatbreads. Pack them into small pita breads together with lettuce leaves, onion rings, sliced tomatoes and cucumbers. Spread with hummus (page 40) or a salsa made from yogurt and harissa (page 95), then fold.

Spinach and feta tart

Tasty when eaten hot, lukewarm, or cold

Serves 4–6:

2 pounds spinach, salt

1 large onion, 2 garlic cloves

2 tablespoons olive oil

freshly ground pepper

freshly grated nutmeg

1 bunch scallions

1 bunch parsley or dill

1/2 pound feta cheese

1/2 cup milk or yogurt

3 eggs

3 large leaves yufka pastry

1/2 stick melted butter

1 egg yolk and 1 tablespoon

milk for brushing

1 Fill the sink with cold water, chuck in the spinach, and swish it from side to side. Lift it out, and wash in more changes of water until the water stays clean. Sort out and discard yellow and wilting leaves, and pinch off any very thick stalks.

2 Fill a large saucepan to one-third with water and place it on top of the stove. Bring to a boil, and add salt. Put the spinach into the water and cook for only about 1–2 minutes, or until the leaves collapse. Drain the spinach into a colander and refresh under cold water. Drain spinach well, squeeze out a little, then chop.

3 Peel and finely chop onion and garlic. Heat the oil in a skillet. Fry onion and garlic in the oil over a medium heat for a few minutes. Add the spinach and continue frying for a few minutes. If a lot of liquid appears, cook to reduce a little. Season the spinach with salt, pepper, and nutmeg.

4 Cut the root ends off the scallions. Wash and slice them into rings. Wash the parsley or dill and shake dry. Pull off the leaves and finely chop them. Stir onions and herbs into the spinach. Crumble the feta cheese, then purée together with the milk or yogurt until smooth. Add the eggs and stir to combine well.

5 Preheat the oven to 350 °F (convection ovens without preheating to 325 °F). Carefully separate the pastry leaves. Thinly brush each leaf with butter. Pile the pastry leaves on top of each other and place them in a springform pan (11 inch diameter) or in a heatproof dish—leave the edges of the pastry leaves to hang over the edge of the dish.

6 Combine the spinach with the cheese mixture, then spread it over the pastry leaves. Smooth the top and fold the overhanging pastry edges over to cover.

7 Put the tart into the oven (center) and bake for just under 1 hour, or until it is nicely browned. After half the baking time, stir together the egg yolk and the milk and brush the tart with the mixture. Leave to stand for at least 10 minutes before serving. Cut into wedges to serve.

Time you need: 40 minutes
(+ 1 hour baking)
Goes well with: tomato salad
with onions and olives
Calories per portion: 360

Variation:

Meat tart

To make the filling, fry onion and garlic as described above. Add 1 pound ground meat (beef or lamb) and fry until it separates. Season with sweet paprika, salt, pepper, and 1 pinch cinnamon. Wash, trim, and finely chop 1 bunch parsley and 1 bunch scallions. Stir into the meat. To make the sauce, stir 1 cup milk or yogurt into 3 eggs, season to taste with salt and pepper. Place pastry leaves into the dish, meat on top. Pour over the egg-milk-mixture and fold over the pastry edges. Bake as above.

Green eggy pancakes

Fresh as a spring day

Serves 4 as a snack or

2 as an entrée:

1/2 pound spinach

1/4 bunch each parsley, dill, and mint

1 leek, 6 eggs

salt, freshly ground pepper

1/4 teaspoon ground turmeric

1 teaspoon dried oregano

4 tablespoons olive oil

To serve:

1 cup yogurt, salt, herbs

1 Fill the sink with cold water, throw in the spinach, and swish it around in the water. Lift it out and repeat washing until the water stays clean. Fish out the leaves and discard any wilted or yellow ones. Finally pinch out any very thick stalks. Drain the spinach in a colander.

2 Wash the herbs and shake dry. Pull off the leaves. Cut off the root end and the dark-green wilted parts the leek. Slit the leek open lengthwise and wash very thoroughly, including in between the leaves. Roughly

chop the leek. Put the spinach, herbs, and leek into a food processor and purée until you have a smooth paste.

3 Crack the eggs into a bowl. Season with salt, pepper, turmeric, and oregano, and beat everything with a whisk. Add the puréed herb mixture and stir well to combine.

4 Place a skillet on the stove with the oil. Pour the batter into the pan and cook over a medium heat for about 10 minutes, or until the surface has set as well as the base. Let the pancake glide out onto a plate—this works best if you use a nonstick skillet—then tip it back into the pan upside down. Cook for another 5 minutes or so. Put the pancake onto a large plate, cut it in slices, and serve garnished with some salted yogurt and a few fresh leaves of herbs.

Time you need: 40 minutes
Goes well with: flatbread
Calories per portion: 555

Easy version:

Grease a heatproof dish. Pour in the egg mixture and bake it in the oven (center) at 400 °F (convection oven 350 °F) for about 35 minutes.

Zucchini pancakes

Vegetarian, crunchy, unbelievably good

Serves 4 as an appetizer or

2 as an entrée:

For the pancakes:

1 pound zucchini, salt

1 bunch scallions

1/2 bunch each parsley and dill

2 eggs, 1/2 cup flour

1 teaspoon hot paprika

freshly ground pepper

4 tablespoons olive oil

For the yogurt:

1/2 bunch mint, 1 tomato, 2 garlic cloves

1 1/3 cups yogurt (sheep milk yogurt is best)

1 tablespoon olive oil

1 tablespoon lemon juice

salt, freshly ground pepper

1 Wash, then cut the ends off the zucchini. Finely grate zucchini on a grater (or use a food processor with a grating attachment). Put zucchini into a bowl, add the salt, and leave to stand for about 15 minutes.

70

2 In the meantime prepare the scallions. Remove the root ends, then wash and chop the scalions very finely. Wash the parsley and the dill and shake dry. Pinch off any thick stalks, finely chop the remainder.

3 Some liquid will have collected in the bowl with the zucchini. Tip the zucchini into a colander and squeeze with your hands to remove as much liquid as possible. Return the zucchini to the bowl. Add scallions, parsley, dill, eggs, flour, paprika, and pepper, and stir well to combine.

4 For the yogurt, wash the mint and shake dry. Pull off the leaves and finely chop them. Wash and finely dice the tomato, removing the stem ends. Peel the garlic and crush it into the yogurt. Add mint, tomato, olive oil, and lemon juice. Season to taste with salt and pepper.

5 Cook the zucchini pancakes. Heat the oil in a skillet. With a tablespoon, place small dollops of the batter into the skillet, flatten them slightly, and fry them over a medium heat for about 4 minutes on each side. When all pancakes are cooked, serve them with the yogurt.

Time you need: 40 minutes
Goes well with: flatbread and a few black olives
Calories per portion: 565

Potato cakes
Good hot or cold

Serves 4:
1 pound waxy potatoes
salt
2 onions
6 tablespoons oil
1 large bunch parsley
1/2 teaspoon each ground turmeric and ground pepper
1/4 teaspoon freshly grated nutmeg
1 pinch cinnamon
4 eggs
1 lemon

1 Peel and wash the potatoes, then cut them into large dice. Put them into a saucepan with salted water and bring to a boil. Cover with the lid and cook them over a medium heat for about 20 minutes, or until soft. Drain.

2 While the potatoes are cooking, peel and finely dice the onions. In a frying pan, heat 2 tablespoons of oil. Stir in the chopped onion, and sweat gently over a low heat for about 10 minutes. Stir occasionally.

3 Wash the parsley and shake dry. Pull off the leaves and finely chop them. Put the potatoes into a shallow bowl and mash with a fork to a fine purée. Stir in the parsley and the onions. Season with salt, turmeric, pepper, nutmeg, and cinnamon. Stir well to combine. Crack the eggs and whisk lightly, then stir them into the potato mixture.

4 Heat the remaining oil in a skillet. Add the potato mixture and smooth the top. Cook over a low heat, uncovered, for about 10 minutes.

5 Now there's a choice of two endings: Either let the potato cake slide out of the pan onto a plate, and then tip it back in the pan, upside down. Cook the other side for another 8 minutes or so.
Or heat the broiler and grill the potato cake in its pan at a sufficient distance from the broiling elements for about 10 minutes, or until the top is nicely browned. For this version, you need a skillet that is ovenproof, including its handle.
For both endings: Remove from the skillet and enjoy straight away!

Time you need: 50 minutes
Goes well with: olives and fery tomato salad (page 49)
Calories per portion: 300

Vegetables

Delicious—without meat

& Legumes

How do you know there's a terrific vegetable store nearby before you've actually seen one? From all the women and men you meet, several blocks before you get there, loaded down with bags full of greens, in their arms a huge bunch of parsley, enough for a two-gallon vase. And how do you realize that this is the store they've come from? Because you can't even see it at first, there are so many vegetables piled so high in front.

Apart from its well-known exports such as doner and shish kebabs, pita bread and such like, the Oriental cuisine is first and foremost a cuisine of vegetables. Here eggplant is braised, slowly and gently, until soft, spinach is combined with raisins and pine nuts, and even potatoes taste completely different from our usual dishes. And there is even more variety and difference with legumes. They don't ever taste like an inexpensive Sunday night meal here—is that because they're on the menu every single day of the week?

What the Orient drinks
Yogurt and water

We've seen great variety in the chiller cabinets: yogurt combined with the most exotic of fruits, with crunchy nibbles, or with assorted lactic acids. But yogurt with water? What's supposed to be so good about that? Known as *ayran* in Turkey or *doogh* in Iran, it's one of the best ways of quenching your thirst on a hot day and of putting out the fire on your tongue after you've eaten something very hot and spicy. Besides, it's the classic drink to accompany an authentic lamb kebab and other grilled meats.

The recipe is as basic as the ingredients: Whisk or blend plain natural yogurt (a firm type is best) with some ice-cold water, season with 1 pinch salt, then transfer it to a large glass—on the rocks, if you want it really cold. Depending on your personal preferences, the drink could be fairly thin (half and half yogurt and water) or thick (4 parts yogurt to 1 part water), or you could add sparkling mineral water instead. For a delicate flavor, add a few drops of rose or orange flower water, freshly chopped mint or basil, as well as freshly ground pepper, freshly grated nutmeg, or ground cardamom. Or sprinkle all these on top at the end. Less common but equally good is a sweet version, where ayran is whisked with a sweetener such as honey, fruit syrup (e.g. grape, fig, or tamarind), or cane sugar and seasoned with 1 pinch cinnamon.

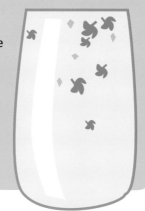

Lentils
instead of...

...lamb

"No meat from a pig!" is the maxim for pious Muslims and Jews alike, because this animal is considered unclean. The reasons for this are that pork fat spoils more quickly in the heat of the desert and that pork—unlike the meat of beef, veal, or lamb—needs to be well cooked so we do not get ill from it. But quite apart from this edict from the Koran (which also applies to animals of prey, reptiles, and insects), meat was only rarely eaten in the original Bedouin diet.

Nomadic tribes, especially in the barren inland steppes, always lived on a mainly vegetarian diet because they needed to keep their cattle to work the fields. Instead they obtained the necessary protein from legumes and dried fish. In order to introduce fats to their diet, nuts, almonds, or sesame seeds were occasionally added to the meal. According to the Old Testament, everyone was entirely vegetarian right up until the Deluge—God gave Noah a special dispensation to eat meat on the Ark. (Is this why the dinosaurs died out?)

Today, meat is still a luxury in traditional Oriental cooking, served only on special occasions. Many recipes can easily be prepared in a meatfree version. For the urban middle classes this is only rarely an issue today as cool storage warehouses provide an affordable supply of fresh meats every day from all the regions, slaughtered according to the rules of Islam or the Jewish religion. In addition, it is taken as law to show respect for God's gifts, and so nothing is ever thrown away. And that is why there is a recipe for everything in the Orient, from a lamb's tongue to a bull's testicles.

On fasting

Wise djin!

The other day, I met a friend of a friend, and told him of my impending visit. He congratulated me and said: "But make sure to visit him after sunset, so that you may not lack in any food." Hmmm. Do they always eat in the dark?

"I have a grandad, very long—this is true—who gives me thirty grapes every year. If I eat the white ones, it is a sin; if I eat the black ones, it is a good deed!" A little djin told me about this saying, just before my first Ramadan—the ancient ritual of not eating anything in daylight, only between sunset and sunrise, thirty times a year. As soon as a black thread can be distinguished from a white one in the morning dusk, so goes the custom, the Muslim refuses all food, drink, and intercourse during Ramadan. He does not do so for any health reasons or because he didn't deserve any better. He simply observes the duty of self-denial so that he might be cleansed in order to see God's revelations.

As soon as the sun sets, the fasting is broken with a swig of water and a few dates, and then supper follows. Before, the woman of the house has set out the rich meal that she prepared in the afternoon so that the dishes too might be praise to Allah. Then all sit down together, often for hours, to eat, sing, pray, recite, meditate, and celebrate, both piously and merrily. The final meal is taken twenty minutes before the early-morning prayer, before the night approaches its end, and the black and the white threads are once again distinct.

Garbanzo snacks

Peanuts are handed out with the drinks in every proper cocktail bar. In the Orient, however, people like to eat *mezze* [appetizers] with their tea, for example deep-fried garbanzos—just like peanuts. And so we've created our very own Basics term for this book, and we'll call them "garbanzo bites"...

To serve 6, soak 3 cups dried garbanzos in plenty of water for at least 6 hours. Then drain and pat dry well. Now fill a saucepan to three quarters with deep-frying oil and heat to 350 °F. You can check the temperature with a wooden spoon: Hold it into the saucepan and if a lot of small bubbles form around its handle immediately, the oil is ready. Put a slotted spoon full of garbanzos into the oil, deep-fry for about 3 minutes, take out, drain, and pat dry. Deep-fry the remaining garbanzos in the same way. Sprinkle the garbanzo snacks with a mixture of 1/2 teaspoon each sweet paprika, ground cumin, and salt as well as 1/4 teaspoon Cayenne pepper and shake well. Leave to cool, then nibble away.

What does it mean...
...halal?

Let's start with the opposite of "halal," namely with "haram." If this reminds you of the harem, you are not even that wrong. If that makes you think of one thing only, however, you would be entirely wrong. "Harem" in Islam is, very generally, any forbidden area, whether these are rooms in the house that are only accessible to women, or places that can only be visited by Muslims. For the rest of the world these areas are "haram," meaning forbidden according to the rules of Islam. Pork and alcohol are *haram*, even fruit gums if they contain gelatine which may be made from pork bones. And "halal" is everything that is permitted according to Islamic law—meat from good animals that have been ritually slaughtered, or the nighttime meal during Ramadan. If you wish to observe this closely, you can find a ruling for all situations in life from books and websites. But if you are about to starve, you may eat the forbidden, anything else would be an affront against life—and thus "haram."

Imam Bayildi

Not only the
learned man
will faint
in ecstasy

Serves 4 as a vegetarian main course
or 8 as an appetizer:

4 longish eggplants (about 2 pounds)

salt

2 large onions

4 garlic cloves

10 ounces tomatoes

1 bunch parsley

1/2 bunch dill

10 tablespoons olive oil

freshly ground pepper

1 teaspoon sugar

1 tiny pinch cinnamon

4 pickled banana peppers (medium hot)

1 Wash the eggplants, cut off the stem
ends. Peel the eggplants to make a zebra
pattern, that is, peel off a 1/3 inch-wide strip,
then leave a strip of 1/3 inch, repeat until the
pattern becomes visible. Place the eggplants
in a bowl with salted water, and leave them
to float in the water until you have prepared
the remaining ingredients.

2 Peel and halve the onions, then cut them
into thin strips. Also peel the garlic and cut it
first into slices, then into slivers.

3 Cut the stem ends from the tomatoes.
Pour over boiling water and leave to stand
for a short while, then refresh the tomatoes
under cold water. Skin the tomatoes and
finely dice the tomato flesh. Wash the herbs
and shake dry, remove the thick stalks, chop
the leaves.

4 In a skillet, heat 2 tablespoons oil. Fry the onions and garlic over a medium heat for a few minutes, or until transparent, stirring occasionally. Do not let them burn. Transfer onions to a bowl, add tomatoes and herbs, then season everything with salt, pepper, sugar, and cinnamon.

5 Drain the eggplants and pat them dry with paper towels. Heat another 4 tablespoons oil in a Dutch oven and fry the eggplants for about 5 minutes, turning them over a few times so they fry evenly all over. Remove the eggplants form the oil using two spoons.

6 Deeply cut each eggplant between two adjacent peeled strips (they are only separated by one unpeeled strip), bend them apart a little, then fill them with the onion-tomato-mixture.

7 Place the eggplants in the Dutch oven, filling side facing up. Place 1 banana pepper on top of each eggplant and drizzle with the remaining oil. If any of the filling is left over, distribute it around the eggplants.

8 Pour 2/3 cup water into the side of the Dutch oven. Cover with a lid and simmer the eggplants over a medium to low heat for about 45 minutes (the liquid should simmer only very slightly—check occasionally). Allow eggplants to get properly soft. Leave to cool in the cooking liquid, then serve.

Time you need: 35 minutes
(+ 45 minutes braising)
Goes well with: flatbread
and lemon wedges
Calories per portion: 395

Eggplants with tomatoes and pomegranates

Looks impressive?
Not really. Delicious?
Absolutely!

Serves 4 as a side dish:

2 eggplants (about 1 1/2 pounds)

1 pound tomatoes

2 onions

1 pomegranate

2 tablespoons olive oil

2 garlic cloves

1 tablespoon grenadine (pomegranate syrup)

salt, freshly ground pepper

2 tablespoons walnut pieces

4 stalks mint

1 Preheat the oven to 480 °F (convection oven to 425 °F). Wash and trim the eggplants, then prick a few times with the tip of a sharp knife. Place them on a cookie sheet and bake in the oven (center) for about 30 minutes, or until it is very easy to push in a knife or fork.

2 Meanwhile, cut the stem ends from the tomatoes. Pour boiling water over the tomatoes, leave to stand for a short while, refresh under cold water, then pull the skin off the tomatoes and cut the flesh into small dice. Peel the onions and grate them with a vegetable grater. Halve the pomegranate and press the juice into a citrus squeezer.

3 Leave the baked eggplants to cool until you can touch them. Cut them open lengthwise and scrape the flesh away from the skins. Dice the eggplant flesh.

4 Heat the oil in a skillet. Stir in the onions and fry for a few minutes, or until they no longer look raw. Peel and crush the garlic.

5 Combine the eggplants and tomatoes, stir in the pomegranate juice, and season to taste with grenadine, salt, and pepper. Sweat over a low heat for about 15 minutes.

6 Finely chop the walnuts and dry-roast briefly in a skillet. Wash the mint and shake dry, pull off the leaves and finely chop them. Combine the mint with the walnuts. Check and adjust the seasoning of the eggplants and sprinkle them with the nut and mint mixture, then serve.

Time you need: 50 minutes
Goes well with: shish kebab
(page 124), grilled lamb chops,
fish fillet with sesame sauce (page 139)
or any rice dish
Calories per portion: 145

Spinach with raisins and pine nuts
The perfect combo

Serves 4 as a side dish or
2 as an entrée:

1 1/2 pounds spinach

salt

1 bunch scallions

4 garlic cloves

1 piece red chili

4 tablespoons olive oil

1/3 cup pinenuts

1/4 cup raisins

1/2 teaspoon ground cilantro

freshly ground pepper

1 tablespoon lemon juice

1 Fill the sink with cold water. Throw in the spinach, and swish it around to clean, then drain. Repeat until the water stays clean.

2 Fill a large saucepan about one-third with water and place on the stove. Bring the water to a boil and add salt. Add the spinach, push it under water with a wooden spoon. Simmer

for 1–2 minutes, or until the leaves collapse. Tip into a colander, and refresh under plenty of cold running water. Drain the spinach.

3 Cut the root ends off the scallions. Wash and trim the scallions and cut them into thin rings. Peel and finely chop the garlic. Wash the chili piece and finely chop it, retaining the seeds (remove seeds if you don't like your food too hot).

4 Heat the olive oil in a skillet. Add the pine nuts and fry until they are a golden color. Add the onions, garlic, chili, and the raisins, and continue frying briefly. Stir in the spinach, season to taste with cilantro, pepper, salt, and lemon juice. Cook, stirring all the time, until everything is heated through. Transfer to a serving bowl and place on the table.

Time you need: 30 minutes
Goes well with: oven-roast lamb (page 120), shish kebabs (page 124), or Oriental fried chicken (page 115)
Calories per portion: 220

Or try this:
Use dried apricots, dates, or prunes instead of the raisins, cutting these into dice or strips. Instead of pine nuts, you can also use almonds.

Zucchini with chermoula
Superb taste and virtually no effort

Serves 4 as a side dish or appetizer:

1 bunch each parsley and cilantro

1 red or white onion

4 garlic cloves

1 tablespoon sweet paprika

1 teaspoon hot paprika

1/2 tablespoon ground cumin

1 teaspoon freshly ground pepper

1 teaspoon ras-el-hanout (page 113)

salt

2 tablespoons lemon juice

4 tablespoons olive oil

1 1/2 pounds young zucchini

1 Wash the herbs and shake dry. Discard any thick stalks. Pull off the leaves and finely chop them. Peel the onion and garlic and cut them into very fine dice.

2 Make the chermoula sauce: Combine the onion and garlic with all the spices, lemon juice, and olive oil, stirring well.

78

3 Wash the zucchini and cut off the ends. Slice lengthways into slices about 1/4 inch thick. Combine zucchini with the sauce, stir, and leave to marinate for about 30 minutes.

4 Preheat the oven to 350 °F (convection oven to 325 °F). Place the zucchini on a cookie sheet or in an ovenproof dish, overlapping a little bit. Bake in the oven (center) for about 40 minutes, or until still firm to the bite. You can eat this dish hot or cold.

Time you need: 25 minutes
(+ 30 minutes marinating and
40 minutes baking)
Goes well with: flatbread, if the zucchini are eaten as an appetizer, or with poultry, fried fish, or oven-roast lamb (page 120) if they are served as a side dish
Calories per portion: 130

Or try this:
Instead of baking the zucchini in the oven, fry them in a skillet over a moderate heat, turning them frequently so they do not burn. Instead of using zucchini you can also make a tasty version of this dish with potatoes (parboil first for about 10 minutes), fennel, celery, or bell pepper—or a mixture of these—and serve it all with a tasty sauce.

Okra with tomatoes
Experiment with pods

Serves 4 as a side dish:

1 pound okra

4 tomatoes

2 onions

2 garlic cloves

1 red and 1 green chili

2 tablespoons olive oil

1 teaspoon each ground cilantro and sweet paprika

1/2 teaspoon each ground turmeric and cinnamon

a few stalks mint and parsley

salt, 1 tablespoon lemon juice

1 Wash the okra. Thinly peel the stems to a pointed tip as if using a pencil sharpener. Don't cut too deeply into the okra flesh, or the juices will start to escape and make the dish very thick and glutinous. If, however, that's what you like, just make a few deep cuts in the pods.

2 Cut the stem ends off the tomatoes. Pour over boiling water, leave the tomatoes to scald briefly, then refresh them under cold running water. Skin the tomatoes and cut the flesh into dice. Peel and finely chop the onions and the garlic. Wash the chili and cut off the stem end. Cut the chili into thin rings. If you don't like your food too spicy, deseed the chili first. (Wash your hands after cutting the chili.)

3 Heat the oil in a skillet with a lid or in a saucepan. Briefly fry the okra, add the onions, garlic, and chili, and continue frying. Combine all the spices, and sprinkle them into the pan. Continue frying, then stir in the tomatoes.

4 Reduce the heat to low. Cover and simmer the pods for 15–20 minutes, or until they are still firm to the bite. Meanwhile, wash the herbs and shake dry. Pull off the leaves and finely chop them. Stir in salt and lemon juice, and serve.

Time you need: 35 minutes
Goes well with: oven-roast lamb (page 120) or Oriental fried chicken (page 115)
Calories per portion: 95

Or try this:
Okra tastes delicious in lamb or beef casseroles, but they're also tasty with braised chicken dishes.

Oriental potato salad
Refreshing and light

Serves 4 as a side dish or
2 as a light meal:

1 1/2 pounds waxy potatoes

salt, 2 onions, 4 garlic cloves

1 green pointed bell pepper (Marmara) or

1 fat mild banana pepper

4 tablespoons olive oil

1 tablespoon black cumin

1/2 teaspoon each ground cumin, ground
cilantro, and sweet paprika

2 tablespoons pitted green olives

1 piece organic lemon zest

1/2 bunch parsley

1/4 pound feta cheese

5 tablespoons lemon or lime juice

1 Wash the potatoes and boil them in
their skins in salted water, covered, for
about 15–20 minutes, or until they are nearly
cooked. Drain and leave to cool a little, then
remove the skins, and cut the potatoes into
1/3 inch thick slices.

2 Peel the onions and the garlic, quarter
the onions, and cut them into thin strips.
Finely chop the garlic. Wash the pepper, cut
off the stem end, deseed and remove white
membrane. Cut the pepper into rings.

3 Place the oil into a large skillet and heat.
Add the onions, garlic, and pepper rings, and
fry over a medium heat for a few minutes,
but do not let them get brown. Add the black
cumin and fry for 1–2 minutes, sprinkle in the
remaining spices, and stir well to combine.

4 Add the potatoes and continue frying,
stirring frequently, until they are completely
cooked. Meanwhile, finely chop the olives
and the lemon zest. Wash the parsley and
shake dry, then finely chop the leaves.
Crumble in the feta, stir in the parsley and
the olive and lemon zest mixture.

5 Transfer the potatoes to a bowl and allow
them to cool to lukewarm. Mix in the lemon
juice and season the salad with salt to taste.
Sprinkle over the cheese mixture. It tastes
delicious lukewarm, and just as good well
chilled.

Time you need: 40 minutes
Goes well with: fried lamb chops, shish
kebabs (page 124), or fried fish fillets
Calories per portion: 255

Spicy potatoes
Deliciously fiery

Serves 4 as a side dish:

1 1/2 pounds waxy potatoes

4 tablespoons olive oil

4 garlic cloves

2 scallions

2 red chilis

1 teaspoon cumin seeds

1 teaspoon ground cumin

salt

a few stalks parsley or

cilantro

2 tablespoons lemon juice

1 Peel and wash the potatoes. Drain and
pat them dry with paper towels, then cut
them into in 1/3–2/3 inch dice.

2 Heat the olive oil in a skillet—if possible
use a cast-iron pan with nonstick coating
that will store the heat and distribute it
evenly. Add the potato cubes and stir well.
Turn the heat to medium and fry the
potatoes for about 15 minutes, or until they
are almost cooked, stirring frequently.

3 Meanwhile, peel and finely chop the garlic. Cut the root ends off the scallions and wash the onions. Cut onions and their crisp green parts into thin rings. Wash the chilis and halve them lengthwise. Cut off the stem ends and scrape out the seeds. Cut the chili halves into thin strips.

4 Add the garlic, onions, and chili to the potatoes. Stir in both the whole and the ground cumin seeds, and season the potatoes with salt. Fry for a further 5–10 minutes or so, until the potatoes are cooked. Meanwhile, wash the parsley or cilantro and shake dry. Pull off the leaves and finely chop them, then stir them into the potatoes. Season with lemon juice and perhaps a little more salt.

Time you need: 35 minutes
Goes well with: oven-roast lamb (page 120), fish with pomegranate sauce (page 138) or a vegetable dish
Calories per portion: 180

Or try this:
Fry bell pepper strips, eggplant dice, or zucchini strips together with the mixture. Artichokes (use the small purple ones if available) also go well with the potatoes: Clean them as described on page 89, then cut them into eighths.

Eggs in vegetable sauce
It's all in the yogurt

Serves 4 as a main course:

2 onions, 2 green bell peppers

1 small eggplant, 1 red or green chili

4 tablespoons olive oil

1 small can tomatoes (14 ounces approx.)

1 teaspoon each sugar and sweet paprika

salt, 8 small eggs

4 garlic cloves

2 stalks parsley or mint

2/3 cup firm yogurt

1 Peel and quarter the onions, then cut them into strips. Wash the bell peppers, cut them open lengthwise. Remove the membranes and the seeds. Wash and trim the eggplant. Cut peppers and eggplant into small dice. Wash the chili and slit it open lengthwise. Deseed, cut off the stem end, then cut the chili into strips.

2 Heat the oil in a skillet with a lid or a wide saucepan. Fry the onions, chili, peppers, and eggplant for a few minutes.

3 Chop the canned tomatoes and pour into the vegetable mixture together with their juice. Add the sugar and the paprika, season with salt, cover, and simmer over a low heat for about 20 minutes.

4 Remove the lid. Crack the eggs into the vegetable sauce next to each other. Replace the lid and leave the eggs to set in the sauce for 6–8 minutes.

5 Time to make the garlic yogurt now: Peel and crush the garlic. Wash the parsley or mint and shake dry, then chop finely. Stir the garlic and herbs into the yogurt. Season with salt. Serve the eggs in their sauce together with the yogurt.

Time you need: 50 minutes
Goes well with: flatbread
Calories per portion: 335

Variation:

Oriental scrambled egg
Briefly fry 2 chopped garlic cloves and 1 teaspoon each ground cumin and sweet paprika in 4 tablespoons olive oil. Stir in 2 teaspoons tomato paste or 1 teaspoon harissa (page 95). Crack 8 eggs into the pan and leave to set lightly. Season with salt, stir, and cook until completely set.

81

Filled vegetables
A bit of everything for everyone

Serves 4 hungry people:

4 small onions

6 smallish tomatoes

2 young zucchini

2 small eggplants

4 small pointed (Marmara) bell peppers

1 bunch scallions

4 garlic cloves

1/2 bunch each parsley and dill

1 pound ground lamb

1 tablespoon tomato paste

2 tablespoons pine nuts

1 tablespoon raisins

2 teaspoons each sweet and hot paprika

1 teaspoon ground cumin

1 pinch cinnamon

salt

freshly ground pepper

4 tablespoons lemon juice

4 tablespoons olive oil

1 teaspoon sugar or honey

1 Wash the onions and cut off the root ends. Put the onions into a saucepan filled with water and bring to a boil. Cook for about 2 minutes, drain into a colander, and refresh with cold water. Leave the onions to cool. Cut off a slice as a lid, then hollow out the onions, leaving just two layers standing. Very finely chop the inner parts that you have removed.

2 Wash the tomatoes. Cut a lid off 4 tomatoes. Using a spoon, scrape out the seeds together with any tomato flesh. Discard the seeds. Halve the remaining tomatoes and lightly squeeze them to push out the seeds. Discard the seeds, finely chop the flesh of the tomatoes together with the flesh from the 4 hollowed out tomatoes.

3 Wash and trim the zucchini and the eggplants, then halve them lengthwise. Using a sharp knife, cut a cross into the cut ends of the zucchini and eggplant halves and hollow them out, leaving a 1/3 inch thick container. Finely dice the scooped out vegetable flesh. Wash the bell peppers and halve them lengthwise. Remove the stem ends and pull out the seeds with the white membranes.

4 Cut the root ends and any wilting green parts off the scallions, wash, and finely dice the white parts. Peel and finely chop the garlic. Wash the herbs and shake dry. Pull off the leaves and finely chop them.

5 Preheat the oven to 350 °F (convection ovens without preheating to 280 °F). Add the onion, tomato, zucchini, eggplant dice, and the scallions, garlic, and herbs to the ground lamb. Add the tomato paste, pine nuts, raisins, paprika, cumin, and cinnamon, then season with salt and pepper. Mix everything thoroughly until the mixture sticks together well.

6 Fill the hollowed out vegetables with the meat mixture and place them into a large baking dish, side by side. Combine the lemon juice with the olive oil, 1/2 cup water, salt, pepper, and the sugar or honey, stir well, and pour in at the side of the ovenproof dish dish. Bake in the oven (center) for about 1 hour, or until the vegetables are cooked. Leave to cool a little before serving.

Time you need: 40 minutes
(+ 1 hour cooking)
Goes well with: flatbread and
yogurt with garlic and mint; possibly also
with grated cucumber
Calories per portion: 360

Arabic stuffed cabbage leaves

A tasty version of an old favorite

Serves 4 hungry people or
6 less ravenous ones:

1 medium-sized cabbage

salt

1/2 cup fine bulgur wheat

3/4 pound leg of lamb

1/2 bunch each parsley and dill

1/4 bunch each mint and cilantro

1 pound tomatoes

1 onion

2 garlic cloves

1 teaspoon each ground cumin,

ground cilantro, and sweet paprika

1/2 teaspoon each ground turmeric and

chili powder

1 egg

freshly ground pepper

2 tablespoons olive oil

1/2 cup vegetable or meat stock

(or cabbage cooking water)

1 Carefully remove 12 leaves from the cabbage and reserve. Use the remainder of the cabbage for another recipe. Using a sharp knife, cut the thick middle ribs from the leaves so they do not stick out too much. Put about 2 quarts water into a saucepan, add salt, and bring to a boil. Add the cabbage leaves, a few at a time (depending on the size of the saucepan), and cook at a rolling boil for 2–3 minutes or until they are soft enough to bend without breaking. Fish them out with a slotted spoon, drain in a colander, then refresh under cold water.

2 Pour boiling hot water over the bulgur wheat and leave to stand for 10 minutes. Remove the largest pieces of fat from the lamb, cut the meat into dice, then chop very finely with a large, heavy knife, until it looks like ground meat. Wash the herbs and shake dry. Pull off the leaves and finely chop them. Cut the stem ends off the tomatoes. Pour boiling water over the tomatoes and leave to stand briefly. Refresh under cold water, then slip off the skins. Cut tomatoes into very small dice. Peel and finely chop the onion and the garlic.

3 Drain the bulgur wheat, transfer to a bowl and combine with the ground lamb, chopped herbs, 2 tablespoons of the tomato dice, and about half the chopped onion and garlic. Add the spices and the egg, thoroughly mix and lightly knead together. Season to taste with salt and pepper.

4 Open out the cabbage leaves and spread the filling on top, leaving a thin edge free. Turn in the edges, then roll up the leaves like cigars. (If you like, you can tie up the rolls with kitchen thread, but this is not necessary if you place them carefully in the saucepan.)

5 Heat the oil in a Dutch oven—large enough to accommodate the cabbage rolls next to each other. Briefly fry the remaining onion and garlic, add the tomatoes, pour in the stock. Season with salt and pepper.

6 Place the cabbage rolls in the Dutch oven, open side down. Turn the heat to low, cover, then leave the rolls to simmer gently for about 40 minutes, or until they are nicely softened. Check the seasoning of the sauce, then serve with the rolls.

Time you need: 30 minutes
(+ 40 minutes cooking)
Goes well with: flatbread and
yogurt with garlic and mint
Calories per portion: 360

Or try this:

Use boneless chicken breasts or ground beef instead of the lamb. Or use bulgur wheat only (3/4 cup) and stir 1 egg into the mixture. Instead of cabbage you can also use leaves of Romaine lettuce—blanch them briefly, and braise the rolls for 20–30 minutes.

Pumpkin with spinach and dates

Looks great

Serves 4 as a side dish or

2 as an entrée:

1 piece pumpkin (about 1 1/2 pounds)

1 pound spinach, salt

2 tomatoes

2 onions

2 garlic cloves

1/2 cup fresh, juicy dates

1 pinch saffron threads

4 tablespoons olive oil

freshly ground pepper

1/2 teaspoon harissa (page 95)

1/4 teaspoon cinnamon

1/2 bunch parsley or cilantro

1 Cut out the seeds and the fibrous flesh from the pumpkin and discard. Depending on the variety of pumpkin you are using, peel the pumpkin if the skin is hard or just wash it if the skin is soft, and cut into 3/4 inch dice.

2 Fill the sink with cold water. Throw in the spinach and swish it around. Drain, then wash again, until the water stays clean. Discard any wilted or yellow leaves, and pinch off the thicker stalks. Fill a large saucepan with water to a depth of 1–1 1/2 inches and bring to a boil. Add the salt and then the spinach. Cover with the lid and cook spinach for 1–2 minutes, or until the leaves begin to collapse.

3 Drop the spinach into a colander, and refresh with plenty of cold water. Drain or spin-dry very well. Wash the tomatoes, then cut them into very small dice, removing the stem ends.

4 Peel the onions and the garlic. Quarter the onions, then cut them into thin strips. Finely chop the garlic. Cut the dates open lengthwise, remove the pits, and cut the flesh into strips. Stir the saffron threads into 1/2 cup lukewarm water and leave to stand for a short while, or until the water has turned golden colored.

5 Heat the oil in a skillet with a lid or in a large saucepan. Add the diced pumpkin, the onion strips, and the chopped garlic, and fry for a few minutes.

6 Pour in the saffron water, stir in the dates and tomatoes, and the pumpkin. Season to taste with salt, pepper, harissa and cinnamon. Turn the heat to low, cover with the lid, and cook the pumpkin for 10–15 minutes, or until it is softened but still firm to the bite.

7 Wash the parsley or cilantro and shake dry. Pull off the leaves and finely chop them. Stir into the pumpkin mixture and taste. Adjust seasoning if necessary and serve.

Time you need: 50 minutes
Goes well with: Oriental fried chicken (page 115) or shish kebabs (page 124); if served as a vegetarian entrée with couscous and a salad or a yogurt dip. Calories per portion: 195

Or try this:

Use potatoes instead of pumpkin (cook for a further 5 minutes) and add 1 red bell pepper, cut into dice or strips. The dates can also be replaced by dried apricots.

Basic Tip

In late summer, pumpkins and squash are available in many different sizes and varieties, while smallish hokkaido pumpkins may be available all year round. Their great advantage is the fact that not only do they taste good, but the skin is soft enough to be eaten too. For all other types of pumpkin, cut the skin away, a piece at a time, after halving and deseeding the pumpkin.

Chilled artichoke soup
Pleasures of summer

Serves 4 as a summery starter:

about 1/2 pound cooked artichoke hearts
(from a jar, or trimmed and home-cooked
in salted lemon water)

1 1/3 cup yogurt (use one that's not too firm,
or add a little more liquid when puréeing it)

1 1/2 tablespoons lemon juice

1 2/3 cups mild vegetable or chicken stock

1 teaspoon ground cumin

salt, freshly ground pepper

1/2 green bell pepper

1/4 bunch dill

2 scallions

1 Drain the artichoke hearts, then cut roughly into dice. Put into a food processor. Add yogurt, lemon juice, and stock, and purée to a smooth soup.

2 Season the soup to taste with cumin, salt, and pepper and place in the fridge to chill for at least 4 hours.

3 Wash the bell pepper, and halve it lengthwise. Remove the stem end, the seeds, and the white membranes. Very finely chop the pepper. Wash the dill and shake dry, then very finely chop. Cut the root ends and wilted parts off the scallions. Wash the white parts and cut into very thin rings. Combine with the pepper and dill, and season lightly with salt and pepper.

4 Remove the soup from the fridge, stir again, and adjust the seasoning with a little more salt, pepper, and lemon juice. Transfer to plates and sprinkle with a few spoonfuls of the pepper mixture. Put the remainder into a little bowl and serve with the soup.

Time you need: 30 minutes
(+ 4 hours chilling)
Goes well with: warm flatbread
(makes for a nice contrast with
the chilled soup)
Calories per portion: 100

Variation:

Cucumber soup

Peel, halve, and deseed 1 cucumber. Purée together with 2 peeled garlic cloves, yogurt, and only 1 cup stock. Season additionally with a little chili powder, then chill. Before serving, sprinkle with a mixture of roasted almond slivers, chopped parsley, and mint.

Bread and green vegetable soup
Makes you really happy

Serves 4 as a snack:

2 leeks, 2 celery stalks

2 young zucchini

2 garlic cloves

5 cups vegetable or chicken stock

2/3 cup frozen peas or fava beans

salt, freshly ground pepper

1/2 teaspoon chili powder or Cayenne pepper

1 tablespoon lemon juice

1 bunch each parsley, mint, and cilantro

1/2 pound flatbread (one day old)

4 tablespoons olive oil

1 Cut root end and wilted parts off the leek. Halve the leek lengthwise and wash thoroughly, then cut into strips. Wash the celery, cut off the ends, pull any strings. Cut the celery into slices. Wash, trim, and dice the zucchini. Peel and finely chop the garlic.

2 Put the leek, celery, zucchini, and garlic into a large saucepan together with the stock and the peas or fava beans. Slowly heat everything, season with salt, freshly ground

pepper, chili powder or Cayenne pepper, and lemon juice. Turn the heat to medium, cover with a lid, and simmer the soup for about 10–15 minutes, or until the vegetables are still firm to the bite.

3 Meanwhile prepare everything else: Wash the herbs and shake dry, then very finely chop them. Break the flat bread into small pieces. Heat the olive oil in a skillet, add the bread pieces and fry, stirring, until they are crisp.

4 Stir the herbs into the soup. Check and season to taste. Add the bread and serve immediately so the bread stays crunchy.

Time you need: 30 minutes
Calories per portion: 390

Or try this:

Make a multicolored rather than a green soup: Chop red bell peppers and tomatoes together with orange-colored carrots and green spinach leaves, and cook them in the stock. Another good soup ingredient: small, tender artichokes, cut into eighths.

Garbanzo purée

Makes a great hot appetizer too

Serves 4 as a side dish:

3 cups dried garbanzo beans

1 organic lemon

1 1/3 cups yogurt (firm, Turkish or Greek yogurt is best; if you like, use one made from sheep milk)

1 tablespoon sesame paste (tahini)

2 tablespoons olive oil

4 garlic cloves

1/2 tablespoon ground cumin

salt, freshly ground pepper

2 tablespoons butter

2 tablespoons pine nuts

1 teaspoon sweet paprika

1 Put the garbanzos into a bowl and cover with water. Leave to soak overnight or for at least 8 hours.

2 Drain garbanzos and transfer to a saucepan. Add enough water to only just cover the garbanzos. Bring to a boil, then reduce the heat, and cover the saucepan with the lid.

Gently simmer the garbanzos for about 1–1 1/2 hours (depending on their age), or until they are cooked.

3 Preheat the oven to 390 °F (convection oven now to 350 °F). Wash the lemon under hot water and grate a little of the zest. Squeeze the juice. Drain the yogurt. Drain the garbanzos in a strainer, then purée them together with the yogurt, sesame paste, and oil until smooth. Stir in lemon juice and zest. Peel and crush the garlic and add. Season the purée with the cumin, salt, and pepper, then transfer to an ovenproof dish.

4 Melt the butter in a small skillet over a low heat. Fry the pine nuts and the paprika, stirring, then spread over the garbanzo purée. Bake in the oven (center) for about 15 minutes, or until heated through.

Time you need: 30 minutes
(+ 8 hours soaking and
1 3/4 hours cooking)
Goes well with: mixed vegetables,
lamb chops, or fried fish
Calories per portion: 400

Speedy version:

Use 2 cans garbanzos (14 ounces approx.), wash, and drain. Purée with the other ingredients, then slowly heat in a saucepan. Heat the paprika and pine nut butter separately and spoon over before serving.

White bean and meatball tajine
Delicious and filling

Serves 4 hungry people:

2 cups dried navy beans

4 red onions

4 tomatoes

1 green bell pepper

1 bunch each parsley and cilantro

1 tablespoon each ground cumin
and sweet paprika

4 tablespoons olive oil

salt, freshly ground pepper

3/4 cup walnut pieces

4 garlic cloves

1 pound ground lamb or beef

2 teaspoons ras-el-hanout (page 113)

2 teaspoons lemon juice

1 Put the beans in a bowl and cover them with water. Leave to soak over night.

2 The following day, drain the beans and put into a saucepan with fresh water. Bring to a boil. Reduce the heat, half-cover with the lid (leave a cooking spoon sticking out). Cook the beans for about 1 hour, or until they are cooked but still firm to the bite. Tip into a colander to drain.

3 Peel the onions and cut them into eighths. Cut the stem ends off the tomatoes. Pour boiling water over the tomatoes, leave to stand for a short while, then pour off the water. Refresh under cold water and slip off the skins. Chop the tomatoes into dice. Wash, trim, and deseed the bell pepper, then cut into strips. Wash the herbs and shake dry. Pull off the leaves and finely chop them.

4 Combine the navy beans with the onions, tomatoes, bell pepper, half the herbs, cumin, paprika, and olive oil, then season with salt and pepper. Transfer the mixture into a tajine dish or a saucepan, add 4 cups water, and heat. Cover and simmer over a medium heat for about 30 minutes. Check from time to time while cooking to make sure the mixture does not get to dry. If necessary, add some more water.

5 Meanwhile, finely grate the walnut pieces. Peel and crush the garlic. Put both into a bowl, together with the remaining herbs and the ground meat. Season with ras-el-hanout, salt, pepper, and lemon juice, then thoroughly knead everything together with your hands. Shape the mixture into ping pong ball-sized balls.

6 Stir the beans, place the meatballs on top. Cover again with the lid and cook for a further 30 minutes. Adjust the seasoning with pepper and salt before serving.

Time you need: 25 minutes
(+ over night soaking and
2 hours cooking)
Goes well with: flatbread
Calories per portion: 755

Artichokes with pickled lemons
Delicious and different

Serves 4 as a side dish or appetizer:

12 small, tender artichockes
(the purple ones taste best)

2 onions, 2 garlic cloves

1 green chili, 1 large pinch saffron threads -

2 tablespoons olive oil

1 teaspoon each ground turmeric and
ras-el-hanout (page 113)

salt, freshly ground pepper

1 pickled lemon (page 131)

1/2 bunch parsley

1 Pull off the outer dark leaves from the artichokes, until the lighter ones appear. Check whether you have pulled off enough leaves: After you've pulled a leaf off, bite into the space where it was connected with the artichoke. If this is easy, it's ok. Cut the dark tips off the remaining leaves. Peel the stem so it tapers to a point. Quarter the artichokes lengthwise. If you can now see hay-like fibers in the center, cut these out with a knife. This "hay" (the choke) will not yet have grown on very young artichokes.

2 Peel and halve the onions, then cut them into 1/3 inch wide strips. Peel the garlic and cut into thin slices. Wash the chili and slit open lengthwise. Cut the halves into strips. Stir the saffron threads into 4 cups lukewarm water and leave to stand for a short while until the water turns yellow.

3 Heat the oil in a skillet. Fry the artichokes all over for a few minutes, then add the onions, garlic, and chili. Pour in the saffron water, then season the vegetables with turmeric, ras-el-hanout, and a little bit of salt and pepper.

4 Cover with the lid, reduce the heat to low, and simmer the vegetables for about 15 minutes, or until still firm to the bite. Meanwhile, wash the pickled lemon under cold water. Cut into quarters, and remove and discard the flesh. Cut the zest into very fine strips. Wash the parsley and shake dry.

Pull off the leaves and finely chop them. Fold the pickled lemon zest and the parsley into the artichokes and serve.

Time you need: 35 minutes
Goes well with: unleavened bread and lamb chops
Calories per portion: 105

Bean soup with lamb
Fairly easy

Serves 4 hungry people:

3/4 cup each dried fava beans, navy beans, and brown beans

2 onions

1 pound shoulder of lamb (boned)

1 cup pitted prunes

4 tomatoes, 1 organic lime

1/2 cup red lentils or yellow split peas

1 teaspoon each ground turmeric, ground cilantro, and cinnamon

salt, freshly ground pepper

2 tablespoons grenadine (if liked)

1 bunch parsley

1 Put each of the beans into separate bowls, cover with water, and leave to soak overnight. The following day, shell the fava beans. Peel and chop the onions. Cut off the larger pieces of fat from the lamb and discard, cut the remainder into 2/3 inch dice.

2 Put the beans into a saucepan together with the onions and the lamb. Pour in 7 cups water and bring to the boil. Reduce the heat to low, cover with the lid, and leave to simmer for about 1 hour.

3 Halve the prunes and remove the pits. Wash the tomatoes and cut them into small dice, removing the stem ends. Wash the lime under hot water and cut into quarters.

4 Add the prunes, tomatoes, lime, and the lentils or peas to the fava beans. Season with turmeric, cilantro, cinnamon, salt, pepper, and syrup. Cover and leave to simmer for a further 1 hour. Before serving, wash the parsley, shake dry, and chop. Check and adjust the seasoning, sprinkle with the parsley, and serve.

Time you need: 25 minutes
(+ soaking over night
2 hours cooking)
Goes well with: flatbread
and lamb chops
Calories per portion: 490

Foul
Served for breakfast in Egypt

Serves 4 as an entrée:

2 1/2 cups dried brown beans

1 large onion, 2 garlic cloves

2 bay leaf, salt

2 red onions

1 cucumber, 3 tomatoes

3 yellow banana peppers

1/2 bunch each parsley and mint

1 tablespoon ground cumin

2 organic lemons

8 tablespoons olive oil (or a large bottle) for everyone to help themselves

1 Put the beans into a bowl and cover with water. Leave to soak over night.

2 The following day, drain the beans and transfer to a saucepan. Peel and finely chop the onion and the garlic. Add to the beans, together with the bay leaves. Pour in sufficient water to cover the beans by about 1/3 inch. Bring to the boil. Reduce the heat to low. Cover with the lid and simmer the beans for about 4 hours, or until they are cooked to a soft mush. Stir from time to

time, and always add a little water, if not enough is left in the saucepan. The beans should be like a soft potato purée when cooked, but not too liquid. Fish out and discard the bay leaves, season the beans with salt, and keep warm.

3 Peel the onions and cut them into very small dice. Wash or peel the cucumber, halve lengthwise, and scrape out the seeds with a spoon. Finely chop the cucumber. Wash and finely chop the tomatoes, cutting out the stem ends. Wash, trim, and deseed the bell pepper, then also cut into small dice. Wash the herbs and shake dry. Pull off the leaves and leave them whole or roughly chop them. Put all these ingredients as well as the cumin and the olive oil into separate small bowls and place on the table. Cut the lemon into wedges and serve on a saucer.

4 And this is how to eat the dish: Spoon some of the bean mash onto your plate (deep soup plates work best), sprinkle everything with the vegetables, onions, and herbs according to what you like, then season with cumin, lemon juice, and olive oil to taste and enjoy.

Time you need: 30 minutes
(+ soaking over night and
4 hours cooking)
Goes well with: flatbread
Calories per portion: 480

Garbanzos and veal
Warming and very satisfying

Serves 4 hungry people:

2 cups dried garbanzos

1 pound shoulder of veal

2 fresh, juicy dates (if liked)

4 garlic cloves

2 stalks celery

1/2 pound spinach

2 teaspoons dried chili flakes or harissa (page 95)

1 teaspoon dried mint

salt, freshly ground pepper

1/2 cup walnut pieces

2 onions, 1 tablespoon olive oil

1 tablespoon lard

1 Put the garbanzos into a bowl, add sufficient water to cover them completely, and leave to soak over night.

2 The following day, drain the garbanzos. Cut the meat into 1/3 inch dice. Put meat and garbanzos into a saucepan, add 4 cups water, and bring to a boil. Reduce the heat

to low, cover with the lid, and simmer for about 1 1/2 hours, or until the garbanzos are nearly cooked.

3 Halve the dates lengthwise and remove the pits. Cut dates into strips. Peel and finely chop the garlic. Wash the celery, cut off the ends, and pull off any strings. Thoroughly wash the spinach in plenty of cold water, discarding any yellow or wilted leaves. Drain and roughly chop the spinach.

4 Add the dates, garlic, celery, and spinach to the garbanzo mixture, season with the chili flakes or harissa, mint, salt, and pepper, then simmer for a further 20 minutes or so.

5 Meanwhile break the walnuts into small pieces. Peel and halve the onions, and cut them into thin strips. Heat the oil and the lard in a skillet. Stir in the onions and cook over a medium heat for about 10 minutes, or until they are lightly browned, stirring well all the time. Add the walnuts pieces and continue frying for a few minutes. Season with salt and pepper. Sprinkle over the garbanzos and serve.

Time you need: 25 minutes
(+ soaking overnight and
cooking for almost 2 hours)
Goes well with: flatbread
Calories per portion: 425

Red lentil soup
Quickly cooked

Serves 4 as an appetizer or a snack:

1 large onion

2 carrots

1/2 stick butter

2 cups red lentils

4 cups meat or vegetable stock

2/3 cup yogurt

salt, freshly ground pepper

1 tablespoon lemon juice

4 slices white bread

3 teaspoons sweet paprika

1 Peel the onion and the carrots and cut them into small dice. Put 1 tablespoon butter into a saucepan, add the vegetables, and cook, stirring, until the diced onion no longer looks raw.

2 Add the lentils and continue stirring, until they are covered all over with the fat. Add the stock and the yogurt, and stir well to combine. Cover with the lid, then simmer the soup over a low heat for 15–20 minutes, or until the lentils are well cooked and soft. Blend the soup in the saucepan using a

hand-held blender, and season to taste with salt, pepper, and lemon juice. Set aside and keep warm.

3 Cut the crust from the bread, then cut the bread into dice. Heat half the remaining butter in a skillet and fry the bread cubes until they are crisp all over. Stir to make sure they do not burn. Meanwhile, melt the rest of the butter in a small frying pan and stir in the paprika until the butter has become nicely red in color.

4 Ladle the soup into bowls, sprinkle a few bread cubes over the top, then drizzle with the paprika butter to create an attractive pattern, and serve.

Time you need: 35 minutes
Goes well with: flatbread
Calories per portion: 415

Couscous,

Couscous! It even sounds delicious!

Rice etc.

OK, so far most things have been quite familiar. A few dips and salads, plus some unleavened bread and falafel, then vegetables as appetizers and entrées and lentils for the soup. But now we're talking grains!

No, not those in bread and pasta, that wouldn't be anything special. Let's just say couscous! Even sounds exotic! And what wonderful taste. Pure and yet so full of flavor, so filling and yet so light. A real small-scale miracle, that finely rolled wheat semolina, just like the manna that saved the lives of the Israelites in the desert in times long gone by.

But perhaps that was rice, after all? For that is really Oriental too—the Persians especially loved to serve it, having taken an idea or two from their Indian neighbors. By now they've become unbeatable world experts in the art of rice cooking, which actually is more like steaming, but also like frying... oh, just read for yourselves. And find out about bulgur wheat and pasta in the Orient too.

What the Orient drinks
Turkish tea

After the North African mint tea at the beginning of the book we've now reached the Turkish black tea, known as "çay." Traditionally, it is made in a samovar. Water is boiled in its kettle base, and then poured via a tap into a small pot filled with tea leaves. This is then placed on top of the kettle to keep it warm, until the tea has steeped. The tea is now poured into the typical tulip-shaped glasses, diluted with more hot water from the kettle, and served with one or two sugar lumps. Meanwhile new tea is started up in a small pot on top. Thus the tradition.

But since not everyone has a samovar at home, Turkish stores also sell double pots made from aluminum that can be used for this procedure. To make 6 glasses of tea, put 6 teaspoons black tea leaves and 1 pinch sugar into the upper pot, which you have rinsed in hot water. Meanwhile, bring 2 cups water to a boil in the lower pot. Pour one swig into each of the glasses to warm them, then pour the rest over the tea leaves. While a new measure of water is being simmered in the lower pot, the tea is slowly steeping in the upper pot, for about 3–5 minutes. Now empty the warmed glasses, fill three-quarters with tea, then top up with boiling water depending on the strength you like. Wash out the pot, refill it, and start up again. And yes, of course you can do it with a simple water kettle and and ordinary teapot too.

Bread
is...

...sacred

No day, no meal without bread in the Orient—after all, it comes straight from God and may well be the only thing on the table to still your hunger. Whether breakfast, lunch, or snack, at the beginning the master of the house always breaks the bread and passes it around the table. Cutting is clearly taboo, for that would mean attacking God with a knife. But the bread itself often becomes part of the cutlery and, held between thumb, index, and ring finger, it is used as a fork for picking up mezze [appetizers] or as a spoon for dips.

And if a piece of bread drops on the floor, you briefly touch lips and forehead with it, then set it aside to use in other ways. For, respectfully, nothing is thrown away in the Oriental kitchen, least of all the sacred bread. At the same time, none of it should be left over at the end of the day—otherwise it is given to neighbors or the needy; that too is a typical custom.

Or maybe a surprise guest breezes in through the door. Then it is, "Be warmly welcomed, my friend. It is a joy to share our bread and cheese with you." And bread, goats cheese, and watermelon are served, for example, together with a mint tea and pomegranate syrup—just what our dear Djin loves to enjoy on a hot summer's evening. Or straight away an enormous tray full of mezze arrives that the women just happen to have made. And know this, this is just the beginning...

On drinking

My dear Djin!

It's so hot here, and the food is so good. How I would love to drink a glass of chilled wine with it! A Tunesian wine would be absolutely perfect—but of course we can't have that here. Or can we? And who exactly drinks all the raki?

Originally, wine was not foreign to us. After all, it was said to have been the grapes from Asia Minor that were the starting point for viticulture in Europe. The famous Shiraz grape, for example, is a fruit from the Orient. As early as the 14th century the poet Hafis wrote, "I want to abandon myself to intoxication—until I am nothing but the gate through which all the images pass!"

In non-Muslim cultures in the Orient, wine is still part of the meal today. Usually, this will be a young, full-bodied wine, with lots of fruitiness but not too much sophistication, that goes as well with sweet dishes as with savory ones and with spicy food. It may come from Israel, the Lebanon, Tunisia, Morocco. In Muslim countries, freshly squeezed juices or chilled syrup and yogurt drinks are served instead as refreshing accompaniments to a meal. And one drink is even more popular than all of these together: cola on ice.

In the Middle East, aniseed brandies, such as arrack or raki, are traditional, or "mahia" in Morocco. Beer and whiskey too are drunk in the hot weather—that is, if the religion permits this. Otherwise you have to resort to a strong mokka or a bubble pipe.

Home-made Oriental Basics

Harissa

What sambal is to Southeast Asia, harissa is to North Africa—a fire-engine red paste of chilies that tastes fiery to start with and then, a little later, spicy. And so it's a real Basic for cooking spicy dishes. Harissa is stirred into dips, soups, and casseroles, and it goes with couscous like ketchup with fries. You can buy it ready-made in Oriental stores, in tubes or cans—or you can make your own.

Cover 1/2 cup dried chilies with 1/2 cup boiling water and leave to steep for 5 minutes. Dry-roast 1 tablespoon cumin seeds and 1 teaspoon cilantro seeds. Leave to cool, then grind to a fine powder. Now purée the chilies and their water, the seeds, 3 peeled garlic cloves, 3 tablespoons tomato paste, and 1 teaspoon salt, slowly adding 8 tablespoons olive oil while puréeing. Transfer to a jar, smooth the surface, and cover with a little olive oil to seal. Unopened it will stay fresh in the fridge for 1 month.

What does it mean...
...Hajj?

Well, a true Sunni Muslim believer bases his life under Islam on Five Pillars: on his commitment to his faith; on his readiness to help the poor; on daily prayers; on the annual fast; and on his once-a-lifetime pilgrimage to Mecca. This fifth of the Five Pillars is known as the Hajj. For Shi'ites, it is one of the ten Branches of Religion. The pilgrimage takes place during the Islamic month of Dhu al-Hijjah. While in Mecca for the Hajj, pilgrims have to observe certain rules. Men have to wear an *ihram*, a white garment of two sheets. The pilgrims, also known as Hajji, then have to perform various rituals symbolizing the lives of Abraham (Ibrahim) and Hagar (Hajarah) that include walking a prescribed number of times around and between several points and stoning a wall. At the end, they are shaved as a symbol of their rebirth. The faithful who have made the pilgrimage are honored by their communities, and some will take the titles "haajji" or "haahhaah" which mean "honorable pilgrim," although the pilgrimage is meant to express the pilgrim's devotion to Allah, not enhance his social standing. A devout Muslim will orientate his entire life around this spiritual goal; and all of life becomes a Hajj.

95

Steamed couscous

Traditional and extra light and grainy

Serves 4 as a side dish:

1 1/3 cups couscous

salt

1 tablespoon butter or olive oil

1/2 teaspoon ground turmeric if liked

1 First you need to find a strainer that fits the opening of a tall saucepan as snugly as possible. (Once it hangs in the saucepan, there should be as little space as possible between the edge of the strainer and the saucepan. If you make couscous often, it's worth considering buying a special couscous steamer, known as couscousière.)

2 Tip the couscous into a bowl with 1 1/3 cups water and a little salt. Leave to swell for about 1 hour so the couscous can absorb plenty of water.

3 In the saucepan, bring 2 cups water to a boil. Work the couscous in the bowl with your fingers to make it light and fluffy and without any lumps. Pour the couscous into your chosen strainer, then hang this into the steamy saucepan. If there is a gap between the sieve and the edge of the saucepan, close this with a dish towel, so that the steam cannot escape.

4 Steam the couscous, uncovered, for about 15 minutes over a high heat. The steam has to visibly rise through the grains.

5 Pour the couscous back into the bowl, and add 1/4 cup water. Leave to stand for a short while. Stir with a fork, making sure again that it doesn't clump. Replenish the water in the saucepan. Return the couscous to the strainer and steam for a further 15 minutes or so.

6 Pour the couscous back into the bowl, combine with 1/4 cup water, crumble well. Leave to stand for short while and return to the strainer again. Steam for about another 15 minutes.

7 Cut the butter into small pieces. Return the couscous to the bowl, and stir in the butter or oil and the turmeric, if using. Pile the couscous onto a platter and serve.

Time you need: 20 minutes
(+ 1 hours swelling and 45 minutes steaming)
Goes well with: all saucy ragouts
Calories per portion: 265

Cooked couscous

Much quicker and also delicious

Serves 4 as a side dish:

1 1/3 cups couscous

salt

1 tablespoon olive oil

1 tablespoon butter

1 Tip the couscous into a strainer and wash thoroughly under cold water. Transfer to a bowl, pour over 1 2/3 cups water and leave the couscous to swell for about 10 minutes.

2 Transfer the couscous together with the liquid and a little salt to a saucepan, stir in the oil, then simmer the couscous over a medium heat for about 10 minutes, stirring frequently.

3 Finally cut the butter into small pieces and fold in with a fork. Stir the couscous grains well to separate and fluff up.

Time you need: 25 minutes
Goes well with: saucy ragouts
Calories per portion: 285

Speedy version:
Instant couscous is even faster to prepare. In a saucepan, bring 1 1/2 cups water to a boil, add salt. Stir in 1 1/3 cups instant couscous, remove the saucepan from the heat and cover with a lid. Leave the couscous to stand for 5 minutes, then fluff with a fork. Fold in a few butter flakes und serve the couscous. (Make sure you serve the couscous in a prewarmed bowl, otherwise it cools down too quickly.)
Alternatively: First fry the couscous in the olive oil for a few minutes, then pour in the boiling salted water, cover, and leave to swell.

Barley couscous

It's grainier and somewhat more substantial

Serves 4 as a side dish:

1 1/2 cups pearl barley (available at health food stores)

salt, 1 tablespoon olive oil

freshly ground pepper

1 Tip the pearl barley into a bowl, add 1 2/3 cups water and salt, and leave to swell for about 1 hour.

2 In a saucepan, heat 2 cups water. Put the pearl barley into a strainer and hang over the boiling water to steam for 20 minutes. Check out in the recipe for Steamed couscous for exactly how to do this.

3 Return the pearl barley to the bowl with 1/2 cup water, stir, and leave to stand for a short time. Steam for another 20 minutes in the strainer. Combine again with water and steam for a third time for 20 minutes. If necessary, add more water to the saucepan.

4 Finally, transfer the pearl barley to a bowl and stir in the olive oil and pepper. Heap onto a platter and serve.

Time you need: 15 minutes
(+ 2 hours swelling and steaming)
Goes well with: saucy casseroles
Calories per portion: 275

Speedy version:
Use instant barley instead of the pearl barley, bring to a boil with 2 1/2 cups vegetable stock, turn off the heat, and leave the barley to swell for 5 minutes. Stir in the oil, season with salt, and fluff with a fork.

And to serve with the couscous, cook a delicious ragout

see overleaf >>>

Fish ragout
Good with couscous, and with rice too

Serves 4:

1 1/2 pounds tomatoes

1 onion, 4 garlic cloves

1/2 pickled lemon (page 131, alternatively

1/2 organic lemon)

1/2 bunch each parsley and cilantro

1 pinch saffron threads

1 tablespoon butter

2 teaspoons each sweet paprika and ground

cumin

salt, freshly ground pepper

1/2–1 teaspoon harissa (page 95)

2 pounds fish filets (you can use anything

sold at the fish counter—from salmon to

monkfish)

1 Cut the stem ends off the tomatoes. Pour boiling water over the tomatoes, refresh under cold water, skin, and halve. Gently squeeze the halves together, pushing out the seeds, and cutting them off with a knife. Dice the tomatoes and put them into a saucepan. Peel and very finely chop the onions and the garlic, stir into the tomatoes.

2 Wash the pickled lemon under cold water, cut off and very finely chop the zest. (Do not use the flesh.) Wash the herbs and shake dry. Pull off the leaves, reserve a few, and finely chop the remainder. Stir the saffron threads into 1/2 cup lukewarm water and leave to stand until the water has turned a nice yellow color.

3 Add the zest, chopped herbs, and saffron water to the tomatoes. Add the butter and all the spices, and gently heat through. Leave to simmer uncovered over a low heat for about 10 minutes, or until the sauce has reduced and thickened a little.

4 Meanwhile, wash the fish filet under cold water, then pat it dry. Cut into chunks of about 3/4 inch, then place on top of the tomato sauce. Cover and leave to simmer again for about 10 minutes. Carefully stir, and serve together with couscous.

Time you need: 40 minutes
Goes well with: yogurt, with mint
and harissa (page 95)
Calories per portion: 190

Spicy lamb ragout
Classic couscous combination

Serves 4:

1 1/2 pounds boneless lamb (shoulder)

4 tablespoons olive oil

1 1/2 tablespoons ras-el-hanout (page 113)

1 pound onions, 4 garlic cloves

1 green chili, 2 tomatoes

1/4 cup raisins, dried apricots or figs

1 teaspoon ground turmeric

salt, freshly ground pepper

1–2 tablespoons tomato paste

1 can garbanzos (14 ounces approx.

if you don't like them, just leave out)

1/2 bunch mint

1 Cut the meat into 3/4–1 inch pieces. Stir the ras-el-hanout into the oil, then pour over the meat and stir to combine.

2 Peel and quarter the onions. Peel the garlic and cut it into thin slices. Wash the chili, cut off the stem end, cut the chili into thin rings. Wash and very finely dice the tomatoes, removing the stem ends.

3 In a saucepan, layer the meat, onions, garlic, tomatoes, chili, and dried fruits (cut apricots and figs into dice first). Stir turmeric, salt, pepper, and tomato paste into 1 cup water and pour into the saucepan. Bring to a boil, cover, and leave the meat to braise over a low heat for about 1 hour. During this time, check occasionally to see if there's still sufficient water; top up, if necessary.

4 Tip the garbanzos into a strainer and thoroughly wash under running cold water. Add to the lamb ragout and simmer for a further 15 minutes or so. Just before serving, wash the mint and shake dry, pull off the leaves and finely chop them. Check and adjust the seasoning and stir in the mint. Arrange the couscous on a serving platter and ladle the meat on top, or serve both separately.

Time you need: 25 minutes
(+ 1 1/4 hours braising)
Goes well with: cucumber yogurt
with raisins (page 43)
Calories per portion: 500

Or try this:
Cook some vegetables with the lamb: for example carrots or turnips cut into chunks, green beans, or fresh fava beans.

Seven vegetable ragout
Nice and colorful

Serves 4:

3/4 pound carrots

1/2 pound turnips (alternatively 1 kohlrabi)

1/4 white cabbage, 2 onions

1 pound tomatos, 2 zucchini, 1 eggplant

2 red chilis, 1 bunch cilantro

1 large pinch saffron threads

2 teaspoons ras-el-hanout (page 113)

salt, freshly ground pepper

2 tablespoons butter or 4 tablespoons olive oil

1 Peel carrots and turnips, cut carrots into 3/4–1 inch-long chunks. Cut turnips into chunks. Trim the cabbage and cut it into 3/4 inch-wide strips. Peel the onions and also cut them into strips. Cut the stem ends off the tomatoes. Pour boiling water over the tomatoes, leave for a short while, then skin, and cut into quarters. Wash zucchini and eggplant, trim, and cut into 3/4 inch dice.

2 Wash the chilis and cut off the stem ends. Cut the chilies into rings. If you don't like spicy food, scrape out the seeds with a sharp knife first. Wash and shake dry the cilantro, pull off the leaves and finely chop. Stir the saffron threads into 1/2 cup lukewarm water.

3 In a saucepan, combine the carrots, turnips, and cabbage with the chilies, cilantro, and saffron water, then season with ras-el-hanout, salt, and pepper. Add the butter, cut in small pieces, or the oil to the saucepan. Heat everything, cover, and simmer over a low heat for about 10 minutes.

4 Add the remaining vegetables, stir to combine, and simmer for a further 10–15 minutes, or until all vegetables are cooked but still firm to the bite. Check the seasoning and adjust if necessary. Arrange the couscous on a platter, make a hollow in the center, and pile in the vegetables.

Time you need: 40 minutes
Goes well with: harissa (page 95), seasoned with a little lemon juice and olive oil, or yogurt seasoned with harissa and cilantro leaves
Calories per portion: 195

Or try this:
Instead of the white cabbage, use peas or fresh fava beans, instead of the turnips use Jerusalem artichokes or parsnips. At the end, add and heat up 1 can garbanzos (14 ounces approx.) in addition to the vegetables.

Persian crusted rice

Known in its home country as tchelo

Serves 4 as a side dish:

1 1/2 cups long grain rice (e.g. basmati)

salt

1 waxy potato (about 5 ounces) or 4 ounces bread (cut into very thin slices)

4 tablespoons butter

1 Tip the rice into a bowl with cold water and stir around. Drain in a strainer, then wash in cold water two or three more times. Drain again.

2 Now put the rice into a saucepan together with 3 cups cold water and salt, and bring to a boil. Boil for about 5 minutes. Tip back into the strainer, and refresh again under cold water, then drain.

3 Peel and wash the potato, then cut or grate it into thin slices. In a wide saucepan, melt 2 tablespoons butter. Line the base of the saucepan with the potato or bread slices. Heap the rice into the pan like a pyramid. Cut the remaining butter into small pieces and distribute over the rice pyramid.

4 Lay a clean dish towel on top of the saucepan, cover with the lid, and close firmly. The saucepan should be fairly tightly shut. Place the saucepan on the stove, turn the heat to very low (on a gas stove, place a grid between the flames and the saucepan), then cook the rice for about 1 hour.

5 Before serving, dip the saucepan briefly into cold water—this helps to loosen the crust from the edge.

Time you need: 30 minutes
(+ 1 hour cooking)
Goes well with: all saucy dishes, e.g. duck with pomegranate and walnut sauce (page 118) or spicy shrimps (page 140), but also with vegetable ragouts
Calories per portion: 355

Tip:

Rice is cooked in this labor-intensive way in Iran (today's Persia) even when there are no potatoes included in the recipe, simply because this makes it unbelievably fluffy and delicious. So wash and precook it, then add it to a saucepan greased with butter or oil. Cover with a cloth, firmly close with the lid, and cook for 1 hour.

Saffron rice with apricots

Fruity and mild

Serves 4:

1 1/2 cups basmati rice

1 pinch saffron threads

salt

1/2 cup dried apricots

4 fresh fleshy dates

2 tablespoons butter

1/4 teaspoon cinnamon

1 pinch freshly grated nutmeg

1 Tip the rice into a strainer and wash under plenty of cold running water until the water that runs out is nice and clear. Drain the rice in a strainer.

2 Stir the saffron into 1 cup lukewarm water and leave to stand until the water turns yellowish. In a saucepan, bring the rice and the saffron water to a boil with the salt. Cover and simmer over a low heat for about 15 minutes until it it fully swollen and the grains separate easily.

3 Meanwhile, dice the apricots. Slit the dates open lengthwise and remove the pits. Cut the dates into strips.

4 Melt the butter in a small skillet. Stir in the apricots and dates, and cook over a low heat for about 5 minutes, stirring frequently. Season the fruits with cinnamon and nutmeg, then fold them into the rice. Check the seasoning; add a little more salt if necessary. Transfer to a bowl and serve.

Time you need: 20 minutes
Goes well with: all meat dishes with a sauce, e.g. lamb ragout with yogurt (page 121) or beef ragout (page 119)
Calories per portion: 365

Or try this:
Instead of the saffron, use 1/2–1 teaspoon ground turmeric to color the rice. Replace the dried apricots with prunes, cut into small pieces. If you like, add a few nuts or nut pieces—pistachios, pine nuts, or almond slivers all taste nice. Dry-roast in a skillet, then stir them into the rice.

Nutty rice with onions
Grainy and colorful

Serves 4:

1 1/4 cups basmati rice

1 onion

2 garlic cloves

2 tablespoons each pine nuts, blanched

almonds, and pistachios

2 tablespoons butter

1 teaspoon each ground turmeric and

ground cumin

1 pinch cinnamon

salt

1/4 bunch cilantro

1/2 tablespoon lemon juice

1 Tip the rice into a strainer and wash under cold running water until the water that runs out is nice and clear. Drain the rice.

2 Peel and finely chop the onion and the garlic. Roughly chop the pine nuts, almonds, and pistachios. Melt the butter in a saucepan, and gently fry the onion, garlic, and nuts, stirring continuously.

3 Add the rice and stir well. Stir the turmeric into 2 cups water, then pour into the saucepan. Season the rice with cumin, cinnamon, and salt. Cover and simmer over a very low heat for about 15 minutes very gently, until fully swollen.

4 Wash the cilantro and shake dry. Pull off the leaves and finely chop them. Season the rice with lemon juice and perhaps a little more salt, then transfer it to a bowl. Sprinkle the cilantro over the top and serve.

Time you need: 25 minutes
Goes well with: meat and poultry dishes, e.g. stuffed chicken breasts with dates (page 117)
Calories per portion: 350

Variation:

Barberry rice
Pour boiling water over 2 tablespoons dried barberries and leave to swell for 30 minutes. Wash the rice, then precook it in 3 cups salted water, drain. Fry the barberries with 1/2 cup almond flakes in 2 tablespoons butter. Stir a pinch of saffron threads into 1 cup lukewarm water. Add the drained rice, 2 tablespoons raisins, and the saffron water, simmer for a further 10 minutes. Season with salt and pepper.

Rice and eggplant bake
Very easy

Serves 4 as an entrée
or 6–8 as a side dish:

1 1/2 cups basmati rice, salt

2 onions, 2 medium eggplants

1 large pinch saffron threads

4 tablespoons oil

freshly ground pepper

1 cup yogurt

2 egg yolks

3 tablespoons butter

1 Tip the rice into a strainer and wash under cold running water until the water that runs out is nice and clear. Drain the rice.

2 Put the rice into a saucepan with 3 cups cold salted water and bring to a boil. Precook for about 8 minutes. Drain in a strainer, then refresh under cold water, and drain again in the strainer.

3 Peel and finely chop the onions. Wash and trim the eggplants, then quarter them lengthwise. Cut each quarter into slices. Stir the saffron into 1/2 cup lukewarm water.

4 Heat the oil in a skillet. Add the eggplant slices and fry over a medium heat, stirring continuously, until brown all over. Add the onions and fry briefly. Pour in the saffron water, cover, and simmer over a low heat for 10 minutes. Season with salt and pepper.

5 Preheat the oven to 350 °F (convection oven without preheating 325 °F). Stir the egg yolks into the yogurt. Melt the butter in a small skillet over a low heat. Grease an ovenproof dish with about half the butter.

6 Combine half the rice with half the yogurt mixture, then turn it into the dish. Distribute the eggplant slices on top, then spoon the remaining rice on top. Cover with the rest of the yogurt mixture, drizzle with the remaining butter. Cook the rice bake in the oven (center) for 50–60 minutes, or until it is nicely browned on top.

Time you need: 30 minutes
(+ 1 hour baking)
Goes well with: a meat or fish dish
in a sauce or with a salad
Calories per portion: 245

Or try this:
Cut 1 pound lamb into dice and fry in oil until browned all over. Top up with 1/2 cup water, season with salt and pepper, cover and cook for 1 hour. Layer between the rice layers together with the eggplants.

Pilaf with chicken and vegetables
Fruity and spicy

Serves 4:

1 1/2 cups long grain rice

2 tablespoons raisins

1 onion

1 carrot

1 leek

2 tomatoes

1 pound boneless chicken (filet)

4 tablespoons butter

3 tablespoons pine nuts

4 cups chicken stock

freshly ground pepper, salt

1 teaspoon ground cumin

1/2 teaspoon ground allspice

1 pinch cinnamon

1/2 bunch parsley

1 Tip the rice into a strainer and thoroughly wash under cold running water. Drain. Put the raisins into a bowl, pour over hot water, and leave to swell for a short while.

2 Peel and finely dice the onion and the carrot. Remove the root end and the dark green parts from the leek. Slit the leek open lengthwise and wash thoroughly. Cut into strips. Cut the stem ends off the tomatoes. Pour over boiling water, leave to stand for a short while, then refresh under cold water. Skin and finely chop the tomatoes. Wash the chicken and pat dry, cut into 1/3 inch dice.

3 Melt a good half of the butter in a saucepan. Add the pine nuts, onion, carrot, and leek and fry. Drain the raisins and add together with the rice. Pour in the stock and stir in all the spices. Cover, then simmer the rice over a low heat for about 10 minutes.

4 Meanwhile melt the remaining butter and fry the chicken cubes over a medium heat until browned all over. Season with salt and pepper. Add to the rice, together with the tomatoes, and cook everything for a further 10 minutes. Wash the parsley and shake dry . Pull off the leaves and finely chop them. Check the seasoning and sprinkle the pilaf with the parsley, then serve.

Time you need: 1 hour
Goes well with: carrot yogurt with dill or cucumber yogurt (page 43)
Calories per portion: 605

Rice with chicken and cherries
Something really special

Serves 4 as an entrée:

1 1/2 cups basmati rice, salt

1 pound cherries (sour cherries are best)

2 onions, 5 tablespoons butter

2 tablespoons sugar

4 chicken quarters

freshly ground pepper

1 tablespoon oil

1 large pinch saffron threads

1 Tip the rice into a strainer and wash under cold running water until the water that runs off is nice and clear. Drain the rice. Put the rice in a saucepan, add 3 cups cold salted water, and bring to a boil. Precook for about 8 minutes. Drain in a strainer, refresh under cold water, and drain again.

2 Wash and pit the cherries (a specialist cherry pitter is best for this). Peel and very finely chop the onions. Heat 1 tablespoon butter, briefly fry the onion. Add the cherries, sprinkle in the sugar, and cook, stirring, until the sugar dissolves. Add 1/4 cup water, cover, and simmer the cherries over a low heat for 10 minutes.

3 Wash the chicken pieces and pat them dry. Halve each piece at the leg joint. (If you move the legs you can see exactly where the joint is.) Rub the chicken pieces with salt and pepper. Heat the oil and fry the chicken pieces until browned all over.

4 Stir the saffron into 4 tablespoons lukewarm water. Melt half the remaining butter, stir in 2 tablespoons of the saffron water.

5 Put half the rice into a saucepan, spoon over the saffron butter. Distribute the chicken pieces and half the cherries on top. Add the remaining rice and the remaining cherries. Pour over the remaining saffron water. Cut the butter into small pieces and place on top of the rice.

6 Wrap the lid in a cloth and place firmly on top of the saucepan. Steam the rice over a low heat for about 1 hour. Dip the bottom of the saucepan into cold water to loosen the rice crust. Serve everything together.

Time you need: 35 minutes
(+ 1 hour cooking)
Goes well with: mint and parsley to sprinkle over the top and a yogurt appetizer, e.g. spinach with yogurt (page 42)
Calories per portion: 800

Bulgur pilaf
Makes a nice
change from rice

Serves 4 as a vegetarian entrée
or 6–8 as a side dish:

1 1/4 cups bulgur wheat

2 onions

2 garlic cloves

2 pointed (Marmara) bell peppers (or

ordinary ones, in which case use

1 green and 1 red pepper)

1 pound tomatoes

2 tablespoons olive oil

2 teaspoons tomato paste

1 teaspoon sweet paprika

salt, freshly ground pepper

1 Put the bulgur wheat into a strainer, and let cold water run over it. Drain well.

2 Peel the onions and the garlic and cut into fine dice. Wash the bell peppers and cut them into quarters lengthwise. Remove the stem end and the seeds, cut the peppers into strips. Cut the stem ends off the tomatoes. Pour boiling water over the tomatoes, leave to stand for a short while, then refresh under cold water. Skin and halve the tomatoes. Lightly squeeze the halves together so the seeds pop out. Cut the seeds off with a knife. Cut the tomato halves into small dice.

3 Heat the oil in a saucepan. Add onions, garlic, and peppers and fry. Add the bulgur wheat and stir well. Stir in the tomatoes and 2 cups water. Season the bulgur with the tomato purée, paprika, salt, and pepper. Cover and simmer over a low heat for about 20 minutes, or until the little grains are cooked but still firm to the bite. Stir, check the seasoning, and transfer to a serving dish

Time you need: 15 minutes
(+ 20 minutes cooking)
Goes well with: yogurt with cumin
or harissa (page 95) or diced cucumber
Calories per portion: 140

Or try this:
Instead of the bell peppers use zucchini and eggplant. At the end, sprinkle a few cubes of feta cheese, combined with a little grated lemon zest and chopped mint, over the bulgur wheat.

Rice soup
with yogurt
Amazing yet true:
it's tasty when
cold too

Serves 4 as an appetizer:

1/2 cup long grain rice

2 onions

2 tablespoons butter, 1 tablespoon flour

2 teaspoons hot paprika

4 cups meat or chicken stock

1 1/3 cups yogurt (sheep milk yogurt is best)

2 tablespoons lemon juice

2 egg yolks

1/4 bunch mint

salt, freshly ground pepper

1 Thoroughly wash the rice in a strainer, then leave to drain. Peel and finely chop the onions.

2 Melt the butter in a saucepan, stir in the chopped onion. Sprinkle over the flour and the paprika and continue frying for a short while. Pour in the stock and stir well. Add the rice. Cover and simmer the soup over a low heat for about 15 minutes, or until the rice is firm to the bite.

3 Whisk the lemon juice and the egg yolks into the yogurt. Wash the mint and shake dry, finely chop the leaves.

4 Take about 1 ladle of soup out of the saucepan and add this, a little at a time, to the yogurt mixture, always stirring well to combine. Now take the saucepan off the heat and stir the yogurt mixture into the soup together with the chopped mint. Briefly heat again without bringing the soup to a boil since this would make the egg yolks curdle. Season the soup with salt and pepper, and serve immediately.

Time you need: 35 minutes
Goes well with: flatbread
Calories per portion: 270

Variation:

Yogurt soup with meatballs

Use red lentils instead of the rice, and cook the soup as described above. (Leave out the egg yolks, however, since the lentils will make the soup sufficiently creamy.) Knead together 1/2 pound ground beef, 1 chopped onion, salt, pepper, and 1 teaspoon ground cumin, and shape into little meatballs. Place the balls into the soup and leave to simmer for about 10 minutes.

Bulgur soup with lamb
Requires no effort

Serves 4 and is actually quite filling:

10 ounces boneless lamb

2 stalks celery

2 onions

4 garlic cloves

2 bunches cilantro

2 tablespoons ghee or oil

1 teaspoon each sweet and hot paprika

salt, freshly ground pepper

3/4 cup fine bulgur wheat

4 1/2 cups meat stock (you could also use water if you season the dish well)

1 lemon

1 Cut off and discard all larger pieces of fat from the meat. Cut the meat into thin strips. Wash the celery, cut off the ends, and pull off any strings. Peel and finely chop the onions and the garlic.

2 Wash the cilantro and shake dry, pull off the leaves. Reserve a few to sprinkle over the finished soup, and finely chop the remainder.

3 Heat the ghee or oil in a saucepan. Stir in the meat, celery, onions, and garlic and fry for about 5 minutes, stirring all the time. Add the chopped cilantro and the paprika, season with salt and pepper, and fry briefly, then stir in the bulgur wheat.

4 Pour in the stock and heat through. Cover, reduce the heat to low, and simmer the soup for about 1 hour, or until the meat pieces are cooked and tender.

5 Finely chop the remaining cilantro. Wash the lemon and cut it into small wedges. Taste the soup and adjust the seasoning if necessary. Sprinkle with the cilantro and serve with the lemon wedges. This allows everyone to adjust the seasoning to their own taste.

Time you need: 30 minutes
(+ 1 hour cooking)
Goes well with: flatbread
Calories per portion: 335

Manti

Little pastry hats from Turkey

Serves 4:

For the pastry:

1 tablespoon butter

3 cups all-purpose flour + flour for working

salt

1 egg

For the filling:

10 ounces lamb, not too fatty
(e.g. boned leg of lamb)

1 onion

1 carrot

2 garlic cloves

1/2 bunch parsley

1/4 bunch mint

1 dried chili

2 tablespoons pine nuts

salt, freshly ground pepper

1 teaspoon sweet paprika

1 pinch cinnamon

For the sauce:

2 garlic cloves

1 1/3 cups yogurt (sheep milk yogurt is best)

salt

2 tablespoons butter

2 teaspoons sweet paprika

1 To make the pastry, melt the butter. In a bowl, combine the flour and the salt. Add the butter, egg, and about 2/3 cup lukewarm water, and knead until you have a smooth dough. It should not stick to your fingers, but should not to be too dry either. If necessary, work in a little more flour or water to obtain the right consistency. Shape the dough into a ball. Lightly moisten a dish towel and cover the dough with this. Leave the dough to rest for about 30 minutes.

2 Meanwhile make the filling. Cut the meat into large chunks. Peel and roughly chop the onion and the carrot. Put the meat, onion, and carrot chunks into a food processor or blender, and chop very finely.

3 Peel and crush the garlic and add it to the meat mixture. Wash the herbs and shake dry. Pull off the leaves and finely chop them. Crumble the chili. Finely chop the pine nuts. Add herbs, chili, and pine nuts to the meat mixture. Season with salt, pepper, paprika, and cinnamon, and knead thoroughly to combine everything, until the mixture sticks together (like a dough).

4 Knead the dough again, then roll out thinly on a floured work surface. Cut the pastry into squares of about 1 1/2 inches. Place 1/2 teaspoon of the meat filling in the center of each square. Now form the hats: Turn the corners up so that they meet in the middle above the filling. Pinch all the sides together. The hats are ready. Bring plenty of salted water to the boil in a large saucepan.

5 Meanwhile make the sauce. Peel and crush the garlic and stir into the yogurt. Season with salt. Melt the butter in a small skillet and stir in the paprika.

6 Put the pastry hats into the water and cook for about 4 minutes on a rolling boil. Lift out with a slotted spoon and place on prewarmed plates. Spoon over a little yogurt sauce and pour over the paprika butter. Serve immediately so that the cold sauce won't cool the hot manti too quickly.

Time you need: 1 1/2 hours
Goes well with: flatbread
Calories per portion: 345

Variation:

Spaghetti with ground meat and yogurt sauce

Fry 1 chopped onion in 2 tablespoons olive oil. Stir in 1 pound ground lamb or beef and fry until the meat is no longer red. Peel and crush 2 garlic cloves and stir in. Season the ragout with salt, pepper, and sweet paprika. Wash 2 bunches parsley and shake dry; finely chop the leaves. Cook spaghetti until they are *al dente* and drain. Put onto prewarmed plates. Stir the parsley into the ground meat ragout, spoon it over the spaghetti, and top with the yogurt sauce. Serve immediately so the pasta will not cool too quickly.

Basic Tip

You can use ground lamb from the meat counter instead of chopping the lamb yourself. You may have to order this in advance from your butcher. You can also use ground beef instead. If you do, make sure you chop the onion and carrot very finely, if possible using an onion chopper.

Herb pasta with meat
Like a casserole

Serves 4 as an entrée:

1/2 bunch each dill and cilantro

1 bunch parsley and chives

1 handful spinach

3/4 cup lentils, 1 cup buttermilk

2 onions, 4 garlic cloves

1 tablespoon oil

10 ounces ground beef

1 teaspoon ground turmeric

2 teaspoons tomato paste

salt, freshly ground pepper

1 can garbanzos (14 ounces approx.)

1/2 pound rigatoni (short pasta tubes)

1 bunch mint

4 tablespoons yogurt

1 Remove the thick stalks from the dill, cilantro, and parsley. Now thoroughly wash them together with the chives and spinach in a sink filled with plenty of cold water, then drain. Chop everything very finely. Rinse the lentils in a strainer under cold water.

2 Put the lentils and the prepared greens into a saucepan with the buttermilk and 4 cups water, and bring to a boil. Reduce the heat to low, cover, and simmer gently for 40–60 minutes, or until the lentils are cooked but still firm to the bite. Check several times if done.

3 After about half the time, peel and very finely chop the onions and the garlic. Heat the oil in a skillet and gently sauté the onion and garlic over a low heat for about 10 minutes, stirring frequently.

4 Turn the heat up a little, add the ground meat to the onions, and fry everything for a further 5 minutes or so, until the meat breaks into crumbs. Stir in the turmeric and the tomato purée, and season with salt and pepper. Keep warm.

5 In a strainer, wash the garbanzos under cold water, then drain. Add to the lentils together with the rigatoni, season with salt and pepper, and cook everything for a further 10 minutes, or until the pasta is cooked. Meanwhile wash the mint and shake dry, and finely chop the leaves. Stir into the soup, check the seasoning. Transfer the herb pasta to plates, and garnish each portion with meat and a dab of yogurt.

Time you need: 1 1/2 hours
Goes well with: some flatbread
Calories per portion: 715

Pasta with leeks and feta
Speedy dish for busy people

Serves 4:

1/2 pound tomatoes

1 green chili

1/4 bunch parsley

3 tablespoons olive oil

1/2 teaspoon sweet paprika

salt, freshly ground pepper

2–3 leeks (depending on how thick these are)

1 tablespoon black cumin

1 pound macaroni or rigatoni (short tube pasta)

5 ounces feta cheese

1 Wash the tomatoes and cut them into very small dice or chop them, removing the stem ends. Wash the chili, slit it open, cut off the stem end, and remove the seeds. (Wash your hands.) Finely chop the chili. Wash the parsley and shake dry, pull off the leaves and finely chop them.

2 Combine the tomatoes with the chili, parsley, and 1 tablespoon oil, and season with paprika, salt, and pepper.

3 Cut off the root end from the leeks. Slit the leeks open lengthwise and wash thoroughly under cold running water, including in between the layers. Cut the leeks into 1/4 inch rings.

4 Heat the remaining oil in a skillet. If possible, use a cast aluminium pan with a nonstick coating; it will store the heat well and distribute it evenly. Add the leeks and the black cumin. Sauté gently, stirring frequently, over a low heat for 5–10 minutes, or until it is firm to the bite.

5 Meanwhile, bring plenty of water to the boil for the pasta. Add plenty of salt. Break up any long pasta pieces. Cook the pasta in boiling water according to the instructions on the package until *al dente*.

6 Crumble the feta cheese and add to the leeks. Drain the pasta, add to the leeks together with the tomatoes. Stir well to combine. Transfer to prewarmed plates and serve immediately.

Time you need: 25 minutes
Goes well with: a small salad
Calories per portion: 530

Pasta bake
Very, very easy

Serves 4 as an entrée:

2 onions

4 garlic cloves

1 tablespoon olive oil

1 pound ground lamb or beef

heaped 1/2 teaspoon ground allspice
(alternatively ground cloves)

salt, freshly ground pepper

1 can chopped tomatoes (14 ounces approx.)

1/4 cup raisins

1 pound Turkish rice noodles
(these are grain-shaped noodles)

1 bunch mint

3 eggs

3/4 cup yogurt

1 tablespoon lemon juice

1/2 pound feta cheese

1 Peel and very finely chop the onions and the garlic. Heat the oil in a skillet. Add the meat and fry until it is browned and crumbly. Add the onion and garlic and continue frying for a short while. Season the meat with allspice, salt, and pepper.

2 Add the tomatoes with their juice to the meat. Stir in the raisins. Cook everything uncovered over a low heat for about 15 minutes, stirring occasionally.

3 Meanwhile, bring plenty of water to a boil for the pasta. Add plenty of salt. Add the pasta and cook for about 8 minutes, or until *al dente*. Drain into a colander and refresh well under cold water. Drain again.

4 Wash the mint and shake dry. Pull off the leaves and finely chop them, then stir them into the meat mixture. Preheat the oven to 400 °F (convection oven without preheating to 350 °F).

5 Layer an ovenproof dish alternately with the pasta and the ground meat mixture. Stir the eggs and the lemon juice into the yogurt and pour over, distributing it evenly. Crumble the sheep cheese and sprinkle over the bake. Bake in the oven (center) for 25 minutes, or until the cheese is nicely browned.

Time you need: 35 minutes
(+ 25 minutes baking)
Goes well with: a mixed salad, e.g.
Turkish country salad (page 49), but omit the sheep cheese
Calories per portion: 865

Meat &

Let us quickly stoke the fire!

Poultry

We want to celebrate something—a birthday, love, the return of the prodigal son from his last-minute vacation in Thailand. He probably never had a single proper meat dish there, the starveling. So let us slaughter a lamb, and stoke the fire, and sharpen the kebab sticks...

I know, I know, that was a little exaggerated. But in the Orient it is a feast when meat is served, and so it's easy for us to go over the top. Let's us take a chicken, then, from a butcher we trust (and maybe an organic chicken for a tasty treat?). We'll stuff it with lemons and shove it into the oven. That's not too bad, is it?

Or we could go properly Oriental and cook the bird in a tajine, the Oriental equivalent of the chicken brick. Works with a duck too. Or with lamb. The last would be either chopped into chunks or ground. Then it can also be skewered. Or it could be roasted whole (this time without a skewer). Whatever... it'll be sufficient for several prodigal sons. And prodigal daughters!

What the Orient drinks

Almond milk

Does anyone remember blanc manger? Once a trendy dessert in Europe, it could be found on dessert menus until well into the 19th century. The story of the upside-down cream made from ground almonds goes back right to the Middle Ages, and from there quite a bit further still. Its origins are in the Orient where even in biblical times dinner was sweetened with an accompanying drink of almonds and sugar. Today guests are often still served an almond milk drink with a touch of cinnamon by their Oriental hosts.

To make 4 glasses, boil 3 cups almonds for about 10 minutes in water, then drain and pat dry, squeeze to pop them out of their skins, now grind to a fine flour. (You can also use ready-ground almonds, but these don't taste quite so good and are also fairly expensive.) Stir the ground almonds and 1 cup sugar into 1 quart water, cover, and leave in the fridge over night. The following day, transfer to a strainer and squeeze out thoroughly. Meanwhile add 1/2 cup sugar and 1 cinnamon stick to 1 quart milk and bring to a boil, then leave to cool. Finally whisk the cooled milk (without skin!) together with the almond juice and 2 tablespoons orange blossom water. Pour into glasses and dust with cinnamon.

A Wedding

...Persian style

Oriental feasts are legendary for how long they last, how much is eaten, and how great the joy of celebrating is. The greatest private celebration is, of course, a wedding. According to Muslim belief, everyone should celebrate this ceremony and start a family of their own. Each Oriental culture has its own customs. We'll take a Persian wedding as an example here because that revolves around food right from the start.

At the beginning, while the bride is waiting for her fiancé, the *sofreh ard* is spread out in front of her, a precious handmade blanket on which foodstuffs and various symbolic items are arranged. These will include a sugar loaf (more about that later); a platter of breads, farmer cheese, and herbs that will be symbolically distributed among the guests; a basket of eggs to symbolize fertility; a small jar of honey to ensure a sweet future; two sweetmeats which later will be rubbed together above the heads of the newly weds in order to bring happiness and sweetness raining down on them; plus an open Koran. But also a needle with different-colored threads if needed to sew shut a mother-in-law's mouth!

After they have said "yes," the betrothed place a piece of sugar loaf into each other's mouths, and guests throw further sugar lumps, gold and silver over the couple. And then the festive table is revealed. The main foods are different kinds of rice dishes, including the sweet wedding rice dish *shirin pollo* and a wedding "cake" made from cream, marzipan, and nuts as well as skewered meat—frequently an entire lamb or calf. Then we'll dance, and celebrate, and eat, and eat, and eat. How about it?

On eating

Sociable djin!

At last I met your friend in the street and have announced my visit. All he said was, "My home is also your home!" What should I expect now?

I have told you at the beginning of this book about entering a house and greeting a guest, and I will tell you about the right time to do so a little later. Let us now talk about eating at my friend's. Once you have taken off your shoes and been shown to your place on the splendidly embroidered blanket—called *sofreh*—the women of the house will serve you tea and snacks. Relax and enjoy pistachios, almonds, raisins in peace and wash them down with tea. Now you are ready.

Delicious dishes are being laid out until, between the appetizers, salads, soups, rice, fish, meat, and bread, you can no longer see any of the *sofreh's* ornamentation. And the hostess will pile as much as she can of her preparations onto your plate—the more you protest, the more you will be given. Since you are an important guest, from afar and a friend of the djin's, she and the other women of the house may sit down with you (otherwise she would be eating in a side room). No one other than the man of the house will break the bread and pass it to you. Take it and use it to "fork" your food or use a spoon—but never use your unclean left hand. You can expect that your plate will always be replenished before you have emptied it. If after an appropriate time you leave an appropriate amount on your plate, you will be allowed a break—over tea, coffee, sweet pastries, and fruit.

Home-made Oriental Basics

Za'atar, baharat, and ras-el-hanout

These are the names of three popular Oriental spice mixtures. All blends taste best if the spices that go into the mix are freshly roasted, cooled, and then ground with pestle and mortar.

- The North African **za'atar,** which is based on sesame seed, takes its name from Persian thyme (zaatar farsi). For breakfast, you sprinkle the mix over your food or onto bread that's been dunked in olive oil. You will need: 1 tablespoon dried thyme, 2 tablespoons sesame seeds, 1 tablespoon sumac, 1/2 teaspoon salt.
- **Baharat,** which is popular in the East of the Orient, has the flavor of Indian curries and is similarly versatile. You will need: 2 tablespoons black peppercorns, 1 tablespoon cilantro seeds, 1 cinnamon stick (about 2 inches long), 1 tablespoon cumin seeds, 10 cloves, seeds from 10 cardamom pods, 1 nutmeg, 2 tablespoons paprika (sweet or hot).
- **Ras-el-hanout** means "the grocer's blend," and it is as complicated (20 or more ingredients) as the ritual of haggling in a Moroccan bazaar. A simple version has at least 10 ingredients: 1 teaspoon each of ground cloves, ginger, cardamom, mace, nutmeg, black pepper, cinnamon, allspice, turmeric, paprika (sweet or hot).

What does it mean...
...cipher?

While trading with Arabs, the painter, scientist, and merchant Leonardo da Vinci noticed that they were using curious symbols which allowed them to do their sums much faster than he could using the roman symbols of I to X. Today their symbols are known as "Arabic numerals" and have become the basis for every numerical calculation in the world. The Arabs had gleaned them from the Indians, and it was Leonardo who explained their use to the learned men of Europe. The most important innovation was the use of the zero, for now 1, 10, and 100 coul be easily differentiated by the empty circles at the end. *Asifr,* the void, gave its Arabic name *sifr* to the zero, and from this *chiffre* and *cipher* developed. Europeans, unschooled in this art, made the zero stand for the entire system of strange numerals. And they called all ten numerals *ciphers.* And this term is still in use today.

Chicken tajine with olives and pickled lemons
Unusual and totally delicious

Serves 4:

1 meaty chicken (about 2 1/2 pounds)

2 tablespoons lemon juice

salt

3 onions

1 pickled lemon (page 131)

1 pinch saffron threads

2 teaspoons ground turmeric

4 tablespoons olive oil

2 teaspoons ground ginger

freshly ground pepper

1/2 pound green olives

a few cilantro leaves

1 Wash the chicken inside and out under cold water and pat dry. Cut it into about 8 pieces: Separate wings and legs at the joints (move them to find the joints). Cut breast and back in half using a knife and poultry scissors.

2 Stir 2 teaspoons salt into the lemon juice and rub the chicken pieces with the mixture. Chill for at least 2 hours in the fridge.

3 Peel and halve the onions, then cut them in about 1/3-inch strips. Wash the pickled lemon under cold water, halve, and slice. Crumble the saffron lightly into a glass with 3/4 cup lukewarm water. Leave to stand for a short while until the water has turned yellow.

4 Wash the chicken pieces again under cold water and pat them dry, then rub them with the turmeric. Don't add any more salt.

5 Heat the olive oil in a Dutch oven or a tajine. Fry the chicken pieces until brown all over. Add the onions and the pickled lemon, alternating chicken, lemon slices, and onions in the pan—too much pickled lemon in one spot would season that part too strongly. Pour in the saffron water and season with ginger and pepper. Cover with a lid, and gently simmer the chicken over a low heat for about 45 minutes. Check occasionally during the cooking time and add more water if the mixture seems too dry. Stir in the olives and simmer for a further 5–10 minutes. Check and adjust the seasoning.

6 Meanwhile preheat the broiler. Take out all chicken pieces and place them on top in the Dutch oven. Put it under the broiler, about 4 inches below the heating elements, and broil until nice and crisp. Sprinkle with the cilantro and serve.

Time you need: 20 minutes
(+ 2 hours marinating and about 1 hour cooking)
Goes well with: flatbread
Calories per portion: 535

Or try this:

If you like, roast some vegetables with the chicken. Particularly delicious are artichokes (find out how to trim them on page 89). But bell peppers cut into strips and carrots or zucchini cut into thick slices all taste good with the chicken (add them after about half the cooking time).

Oriental fried chicken

This is one we made up for ourselves

Serves 4 (if there are a few appetizers and a dessert), or 2–3 (if nothing else is being served):

1 meaty chicken (about 3 pounds)

1 organic lemon

4 garlic cloves

1/2 bunch cilantro

1 teaspoon each sweet paprika, freshly ground pepper, ground turmeric, and ground cumin seeds

1/2 teaspoon each cinnamon and ground ginger

4 tablespoons olive oil, salt

1 Wash the chicken inside and out, then pat it dry. Wash the lemon under hot water, then prick all over with a fork so the juices can escape during cooking. Peel and halve the garlic. Wash the cilantro and shake dry.

2 Preheat the oven to 450 °F (convection ovens now to 400 °F). Stir all the spices into the olive oil to combine well. Rub the chicken inside and out with salt, then put the lemon, the garlic, and the cilantro into the chicken's cavity. Now brush the chicken with some of the spiced oil.

3 Place the chicken into a roasting pan—choose one that is not too large (see below)—placing it not on its breast or back but on its side. Roast in the oven (center) for about 20 minutes. Now turn the chicken to the other side, brush again with spiced oil, and roast for another 20 minutes. If juices start to collect in the roasting pan, use these to baste the chicken. This will enable the meat to stay moist while the skin turns nice and crispy. (Juices will only collect in a small dish; in a large dish, the juices will immediately start to stick and burn, so they basically disappear again.)

4 After these 40 minutes of roasting, place the chicken on its back, with the legs pointing upward, and roast for a further 25 minutes. Now check whether it is done: Insert a small skewer into the thickest part of the leg. If the juices that run out are clear, the chicken is done; if there is still a hint of red, cook the chicken for a little longer.

Time you need: 15 minutes
(+ about 1 hour roasting)
Goes well with: flatbread, salad
(e.g. orange salad with dates (page 46) or salad with pistachio dressing (page 47) plus a dip such as yogurt with cucumber, hot paprika paste (paste 40), or babaganoush (page 38)
Calories per portion: 440

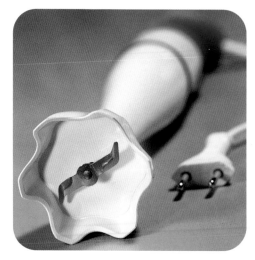

Circassian chicken
One to serve cold

Serves 4 as an entrée or

8–10 as an appetizer:

1 chicken (about 2 3/4 pounds), 1 onion

1 stalk celery, 1 carrot

1 teaspoon peppercorns

2 bay leaves, salt

4 slices white bread

1 1/4 cups walnuts (shellled)

1 teaspoon each hot and sweet paprika

freshly ground pepper

1/4 bunch parsley

2 tablespoons butter

1–2 teaspoons chili powder

1 Wash the chicken inside and out under cold water, place it in a large saucepan. Wash the onion and halve it with the skin on. Wash celery and carrot and cut into large chunks. Put the onion, celery, carrot, peppercorns and bay leaves into the pot with the chicken.

2 Add sufficient water to cover the chicken completely. Bring to a boil, add salt. Reduce the heat to low, half cover with a lid (leave a

cooking spoon to stick out), and simmer the chicken very gently for about 1 hour. Remove the chicken from the stock and let it cool. Strain the stock and reserve.

3 Cut the crust off the bread, place it in a small bowl, and pour over 1 cup of the stock. Leave to soak. Reserve a few nuts for serving and, using a food processer, finely grate the remainder. Very finely chop the soaked bread (use a hand-held blender or the food processor), then combine it with the walnuts to make a smooth paste.

4 Skin the chicken and take the flesh off the bones. Tear the flesh into thin strips. Combine the chicken with the nut paste, season everything to taste with paprika, salt, and freshly ground pepper. If the mixture is too thick, stir in a little more of the stock.

5 Put the chicken onto a platter. Wash the parsley and shake dry, pull off the leaves, and sprinkle over the chicken together with the remaining walnuts. Melt the butter and stir in the chili powder. Drizzle the chili butter over the meat and serve.

Time you need: 40 minutes
(+ 1 hour cooking and time for cooling)
Goes well with: flatbread and
a few slices of cucumber and tomatoes
Calories per portion: 695

Chicken with honeyed tomatoes
Sweet and tasty

Serves 4:

4 large chicken quarters (about 1/2 pound each)

salt, freshly ground pepper

2 tablespoons lemon juice

1 1/2 pounds tomatoes

1 large onion

1 large pinch saffron threads

2 tablespoons oil

1 teaspoon ground ginger

2 teaspoons cinnamon

3/4 cup blanched almonds

2 tablespoons sesame seeds

2 tablespoons runny honey

1 Wash the chicken pieces under cold water, pat dry. Stir salt and pepper into the lemon juice, rub the chicken with the liquid.

2 Cut the stem ends off the tomatoes. Pour some boiling water over the tomatoes, briefly leave to stand, then refresh under cold water.

Skin the tomatoes, then cut them into eighths. Remove the seeds. Peel and finely chop the onion. Crumble the saffron threads into 1/2 cup lukewarm water and stir.

3 Put a Dutch oven or a tajine on the stove. Heat 1 tablespoon oil. Fry the chicken pieces all over in the oil. Spread the onion and tomatoes around them and season with salt, pepper, ginger, and cinnamon. Pour in the saffron water and cover the pot. Simmer the chicken legs over a low heat for about 1 hour, or until the meat is very tender.

4 Halve the almonds and fry them together with the sesame seeds over a medium heat in the remaining oil until they are a golden color. Transfer to a plate. When the chicken is cooked, remove it from the pot and keep warm. Stir the honey into the tomatoes and heat through. Season to taste with salt and pepper. Return the chicken pieces to the pot, sprinkle with the almond mixture, and serve.

Time you need: 20 minutes
(+ 1 hour cooking)
Goes well with: flatbread, couscous (pages 96/97), or nutty rice with onions (page 101), possibly also with a yogurt dip
Calories per portion: 590

Chicken breast with dates
Fruity and tasty

Serves 4:

1/3 cup dried apricots

juice of 3 oranges

1/2 cup fresh fleshy dates

1 onion, 2 garlic cloves

1 teaspoon ras-el-hanout (page 113)

salt, freshly ground pepper

4 skinless chicken breasts (about 6 ounces each)

3 tablespoons olive oil

1 bunch scallions

1 red chili

1/4 bunch cilantro or parsley

1 Very finely dice the apricots. In a bowl, combine the diced apricot with the orange juice. Leave to steep for about 1 hour.

2 Slit open the dates, remove the pits. Roughly chop the dates. Peel and roughly chop the onion and the garlic. Purée the dates with the onion and the garlic in a blender until you have a fine paste. Season with ras-el-hanout, salt, and pepper.

3 Wash the chicken breasts under cold water and pat them dry. Cut a pocket into one side of each, without damaging the flesh too much. Spread the date paste into the pockets. Close each opening with a toothpick. Season the stuffed chicken breasts on the outside with salt and pepper.

4 Heat the olive oil in a frying pan. Fry the chicken breasts in the oil over a medium heat for about 5 minutes on each side.

5 Meanwhile, cut the root ends off the scallions. Wash and cut the whole of the scallions into thin rings. Wash the chili, cut off the stem, cut the chili into thin rings, leaving the seeds in. Wash the cilantro or parsley and shake dry, finely chop the leaves.

6 Cover the chicken breasts to keep them warm. Fry the scallion and chili rings in the frying fat for 2–3 minutes. Add the apricots with the orange juice and bring to a boil. Season the sauce with salt to taste. Arrange the chicken breasts on the plates, pour over the sauce, and sprinkle with the herbs.

Time you need: 35 minutes
(+ 1 hour marinating)
Goes well with: flatbread, couscous (pages 96/97), or nutty rice with onions (page 101)
Calories per portion: 410

Duck in a pomegranate and walnut sauce
Great for any day of the year

Serves 4:

1 duck (about 4 1/2 pounds)

salt, freshly ground pepper

2 onions

2 cups shelled walnuts

2 tablespoons olive oil

1/2 teaspoon each ground turmeric and cinnamon

1 pinch each freshly grated nutmeg and cilantro seeds

8 tablespoons grenadine (pomegranate syrup)

1 Wash the duck inside and out, then pat it dry. Get a sharp knife and poultry scissors ready to divide the duck into pieces. Cut off wings and legs at the joints (you will easily recognize the right spot when you move the joints). Cut the back in half and the breast into four pieces. Rub the duck pieces with salt and pepper.

2 Peel and finely chop the onions. Grate the walnuts in a food processor. In a skillet, heat 1 tablespoon olive oil, and lightly fry the walnuts for 2–3 minutes over a medium heat, stirring constantly, to make sure they don't burn. Transfer to a plate.

3 Heat the remaining oil in a Dutch oven and fry the duck pieces all over. Briefly take the duck out of the pot and pour off the fat that has collected. Add the onions to the pot and fry briefly. Pour in 2 cups water, season with turmeric, cinnamon, nutmeg, and the cilantro seeds, then return the duck pieces to the pot. Cover and simmer over a low heat for about 25 minutes.

4 Stir in the walnuts, then simmer for a further 25 minutes. A thin layer of fat will probably have formed on top of the sauce by now. Skim off as much as you can with a spoon. Hold the spoon straight so that only the fat and not the sauce will run into it.

5 Stir in the grenadine, season with salt and pepper, then cook the duck for another 30 minutes, or until it is nice and tender. Before serving, skim off more fat.

Time you need: 40 minutes
(+ about 1 1/4 hours cooking time)
Goes well with: Persian crusted rice
(page 100)
Calories per portion: 1225

Spicy chicken livers
Quick to prepare

Serves 4:

1 2/3 pounds chicken livers

1 bunch each parsley and mint

1 organic lemon

2 garlic cloves

2 teaspoons ground cumin

1 teaspoon sweet paprika

1/2 teaspoon chili powder, 1 green chili

3 tomatoes, 4 tablespoons oil

salt, freshly ground pepper

1 pinch cinnamon

1 Wash and pat dry the chicken livers. Cut off the little membranes. Wash the herbs and shake dry. Pull off the leaves and chop them. Wash the lemon under hot water, then pare off a paperthin piece of zest and cut this into strips. Squeeze the lemon. Peel and finely chop the garlic.

2 Stir the herbs, garlic, cumin, paprika, and chili powder into the lemon juice. Add the livers and stir to coat all over. Leave to marinate for a short while.

3 Wash the chili, cut off the stem end, cut the chili into thin rings. Cut the stem ends off the tomatoes. Pour over boiling water and leave to stand for a short while. Refresh under cold water. Skin and dice tomatoes.

4 Heat the oil in a skillet. Put half the livers into the pan and fry for 2–3 minutes, stirring frequently. Remove the livers, and fry the second portion.

5 When all the livers are cooked, put the chili into the pan and fry briefly. Add the tomatoes and cook over a medium heat for about 5 minutes. Season with salt, pepper, and cinnamon. Return livers to the pan and heat through. Sprinkle with the lemon zest.

Time you need: 30 minutes
Goes well with: flatbread or rice
Calories per portion: 340

Variation:

Turkish-style chicken livers

Peel 1/2 pound red onions and cut into thin rings. Combine with 1 bunch chopped parsley, salt, and 1 teaspoon sumac. Coat 1 2/3 pounds chicken livers with flour, then fry for 3–4 minutes in hot oil. Season with salt, pepper, and sweet paprika and arrange on the onion mixture.

Beef ragout
Nice 'n' spicy

Serves 4:

1 2/3 pounds beef (from the shin)

2 onions, 2 garlic cloves

1/2 pound tomatoes

1 tablespoon tomato paste

2 teaspoons sweet paprika

1 teaspoon cinnamon

1 teaspoon harissa (page 95)

2 tablespoons ground cumin

1 tablespoon olive oil, 2 tablespoons ghee

salt, freshly ground pepper

3/4 pound okra

1 organic lime, 1 bunch cilantro

1 Cut the beef into 1 –1 1/2-inch chunks. Peel and very finely chop the onions and the garlic—almost to a mousse. Cut stem ends off the tomatoes. Pour over boiling water, leave to steep for a short while, refresh under cold water, and skin. Halve, deseed, and finely chop the tomatoes.

2 Combine the onions and garlic with the tomatoes, tomato paste, paprika, harissa, cumin, and cinnamon.

3 Heat the oil and the ghee in a large skillet or Dutch oven. Fry the meat in the oil in two portions. Stir in the tomato mixture and cook for about 10 minutes. Add 2 cups water, season with salt and pepper. Cover and simmer over a low heat for 1 1/4 hours. Add more water if necessary.

4 Meanwhile wash the okra. Cut the ends with a knife to a tip, like sharpening a pencil. Do not cut too deeply into the flesh as this would make the sticky juice ooze out. Bring salted water to a boil and parboil the okra for 2 minutes. Refresh under cold water. Wash the lime under hot water, cut into quarters.

5 Add okra and lime to the meat and cook for a further 20 minutes. Wash the cilantro and shake dry, finely chop the leaves. Season the ragout with salt and pepper and sprinkle with the cilantro, then serve.

Time you need: 35 minutes
(+ 1 1/4 hours cooking time)
Goes well with: flat bread
or couscous (pages 96/97)

Or try this:
Do not parboil the okra but add them raw. They will ooze a sticky juice and thicken the ragout.

Oven-roast lamb

Cooks almost by itself

Serves 4–6:

1 pickled lemon (page 131) or

1 ordinary lemon

1 onion

2 garlic cloves

1 bunch each parsley and cilantro

5 tablespoons olive oil

or 2 tablespoons ghee

1 teaspoon dried thyme

2 teaspoons each ground cumin

and sweet paprika

1/2 teaspoon harissa (page 95)

2 1/2 pounds lamb for roasting

(boned leg or shoulder)

salt, freshly ground pepper

1 large pinch saffron threads

1 Peel the pickled or the ordinary lemon so as to remove the white pith too. Cut the flesh into small dice, removing the pits.

2 Peel the onion and the garlic. Finely grate the onion, crush the garlic. Wash the parsley and the cilantro and shake dry. Finely chop the leaves.

3 Preheat the oven to 480 °F (convection oven now to 425 °F). Combine the olive oil or ghee with the lemon flesh, onion, garlic, fresh herbs, thyme, cumin, paprika, and harissa.

4 Cut the larger pieces of fat off the lamb. In a small bowl, combine about 2 teaspoons salt and 1 teaspoon pepper. Rub the lamb all over with the mixture, then brush with the spiced oil. Place in a roasting pan.

5 Roast the lamb in the oven (bottom) for about 10 minutes. Reduce the heat to 350 °F (convection oven 325 °F), then cook the lamb for about 1 1/2 hours. After about half the cooking time, stir the saffron into 3/4 cup lukewarm water, leave to steep for a short while, then pour into the roasting pan.

6 Let the lamb rest for about 10 minutes before serving, then slice and serve.

Time you need: 30 minutes
(+ 1 hour 40 minutes roasting)
Goes well with: flatbread and
zucchini with chermoula (page 78)
Calories per portion: 470

Lamb ragout with rhubarb

Rhubarb, rhubarb!

Serves 4:

1 1/2 pounds lamb (boned, e.g. shoulder)

2 onions, 4 tablespoons oil

salt, freshly ground pepper

1 bunch each parsley and mint

1 pound rhubarb

1/4 teaspoon each freshly grated nutmeg,

cinnamon, ground cardamom, and ground

cilantro seeds

1 tablespoon sugar

mint leaves to serve

1 Cut off the larger pieces of fat and any sinews from the lamb. Cut the meat into chunks of about 3/4 inch. Peel the onions and cut them into thin rings.

2 In a Dutch oven, heat 2 tablespoons oil, then fry the onions and the meat in it for about 10 minutes, stirring frequently. Add 1 cup water, season with salt and pepper. Reduce the heat, cover with a lid, and simmer the meat for about 1 hour.

3 Wash the herbs and shake dry. Pull off the leaves and finely chop them. Wash the rhubarb, cut off the tops and ends. If there are any strings, pull them off. Cut the rhubarb into chunks of about 1/3 inch.

4 Heat the remaining oil in a Dutch oven or a skillet. Stir in the herbs and briefly sauté them. Add to the meat. Season to taste with the spices and the sugar, then braise for a further 15 minutes.

5 Stir in the rhubarb and cook for a further 10 minutes, or until it is cooked. Check and adjust the seasoning if necessary. Sprinkle with the mint leaves and serve.

Time you need: 30 minutes
(+ etwa 1 1/2 hours cooking)
Goes well with: rice or couscous
(page 96/97)
Calories per portion: 320

Variation:

Lamb ragout with peaches
Instead of the rhubarb, skin 4 peaches and remove the pits. Cut the peaches into wedges. Add to the stew at the end to warm through. Season the ragout with some saffron for extra flavor.

Lamb ragout with yogurt
Really easy

Serves 4:
1 2/3 pounds leg of lamb (boneless)
salt, freshly ground pepper
2 onions
4 garlic cloves
a few saffron threads
3 tablespoons ghee
2 teaspoons each ground turmeric and ground cumin
1 teaspoon each sweet paprika and ground ginger
1/2 teaspoon each ground cloves and cinnamon
2 teaspoons sugar, 1 cup yogurt
1 teaspoon cornstarch
4 tablespoons pine nuts
cilantro leaves to serve

1 Cut the meat into chunks, about 3/4 inch large, and season with salt and pepper. Peel and finely chop the onions and the garlic. Stir the saffron into 1/2 cup lukewarm water.

2 In a Dutch oven, heat 2 tablespoons ghee, and briefly fry the onions and garlic in it. Add the meat and brown all over. Combine the turmeric, cumin, paprika, ginger, cloves, cinnamon, and sugar and sprinkle in. Fry a little longer until the fine aromas of the spices are released.

3 Add the saffron water. Whisk the cornstarch into the yogurt, stirring to combine well. Season the sauce with salt, cover with the lid, and simmer the meat over a low heat for about 1 hour.

4 Just before the lamb is cooked, heat the remaining ghee and fry the pine nuts until golden brown, stirring constantly so they do not burn. Once they are dark, remove from the pan immediately and transfer to a plate. Check the seasoning, then sprinkle with the pine nuts and the cilantro.

Time you need: 20 minutes
(+ 1 hour cooking)
Goes well with: flatbread or Persian crusted rice (page 100)
Calories per portion: 660

Lamb tajine with quinces
Morroccan classic

Serves 4:

For the meat:

2 pounds shoulder of lamb (with bone; ask your butcher to cut it into 4-inch chunks)

2 teaspoons ras-el-hanout (page 113)

2 teaspoons ground turmeric

1 teaspoon each cinnamon and ground ginger

3 teaspoons sugar

salt

2 onions

1/pinch saffron threads

4 tablespoons olive oil or 1 tablespoon ghee

For the quinces:

4 quinces (1 1/2–2 pounds)

1 pinch saffron threads

2 tablespoons olive oil

1/2 teaspoon each ras-el-hanout (page 113), cinnamon, and ground ginger

1 tablespoon sugar

1 To prepare the meat, rub the lamb pieces with a damp cloth in order to remove any bone splinters. Combine all the spices with 2 teaspoons salt and rub the meat with the spice mixture.

2 Peel the onions, then grate them on a vegetable grater. Crumble the saffron into 1 cup lukewarm water and leave to soak until the water has turned yellow.

3 Put the lamb, the onions, oil or ghee, and the saffron water into a tajine or a Dutch oven and heat. Cover with the lid, then cook the lamb over a low heat for about 1 hour, or until it is so tender that the meat almost falls off the bones.

4 After about 20 minutes, rub the quinces with a cloth to remove the fluff. Cut them into quarters, and remove the cores with a sharp knife. This is easiest if you cut into the quarters from two sides and then break them out. On the outside, carve a cross into each quince quarter. Crumble the saffron and stir into about 3/4 cup lukewarm water.

5 Heat the olive oil in a skillet and briefly fry the quinces. Season with ras-el-hanout, cinnamon, ginger, and sugar, then pour in the saffron water. Cover and simmer the quinces over a low heat for 20–30 minutes, or until they are soft.

6 Check the lamb for seasoning and transfer it to a large plate or serving platter. Arrange the quinces on top of the tajine and serve immediately.

Time you need: 1 1/2 hours
Goes well with: flatbread or couscous (page 96/97)
Calories per portion: 515

Variation:

Lamb tajine with prunes

Prepare and cook the lamb as described above. Instead of the quinces, heat 1/2 pound prunes (pitted) in a saucepan together with 1 tablespoon olive oil, salt, 1 tablespoon honey, and 1/2 teaspoon each ras-el-hanout (page 113), cinnamon, and ginger powder, and 1 cup water. Cover and simmer over a low heat for 20–30 minutes. In a skillet heat 2 tablespoons olive oil. Fry 1 1/4 cup blanched almonds in the oil over a medium heat, stirring constantly, until they are golden brown and crisp. Transfer the lamb tajine to a platter and garnish with the prunes and the almonds. Just divine!

Basic Tip

If you have quite a few friends coming for dinner, prepare double the amount of lamb. Serve with both the quinces and the prunes. To serve, arrange the lamb tajine on two large platters and cover half with quinces, the other half with prunes. Everyone will assume you magicked up two dishes!

Shish kebab
Straight from the skewer or rolled in a wrap

Serves 4:

1 1/2 pounds leg of lamb (boned)

1 large onion, 2 garlic cloves

1/2 bunch parsley, 2 tablespoons lemon juice

1 tablespoon sweet paprika

2 teaspoons ground cumin

salt, freshly ground pepper

4 tablespoons olive oil

1 green and 1 red bell pepper

4 firm tomatoes

4 chilis, if liked

1 Cut off large pieces of fat and sinews from the lamb. Cut the meat into 3/4-inch cubes. Peel the onion and the garlic, finely grate the onion, crush the garlic. Wash the parsley and shake dry, then finely chop the leaves.

2 Combine the onion, garlic, parsley, lemon juice, paprika, cumin, salt, pepper, and oil. Add the meat cubes, stir to coat all over, then place in the fridge to marinate for at least 4 hours or, even better, over night.

3 Wash and trim the bell peppers, then cut them into 3/4-inch pieces. Wash and quarter the tomatoes, removing the stem ends. Halve the quarters again crosswise. If using, wash the chilis, remove the stems, then cut them into 3/4-inch lengths, with or without the seeds, depending on how hot you like your food. Then, if using skewers, thread the meat, bell peppers, tomatoes, and chilis onto them, alternating the items.

4 Heat a broiler or charcoal grill, or heat a ridged skillet on top of the stove. Place the skewers on a rack, then cook for about 15 minutes under the broiler, over the embers, or in the skillet. Turn the skewers from time to time.

Time you need: 1 hour
(+ 4 hours marinating)
Goes well with: flatbread from theskillet (page 61), salad leaves, and fresh herbs. Serve the meat stuffed in pita bread together with the other ingredients.
Calories per portion: 530

Meatballs with rice
Here's competition for Swedish meatballs!

Serves 4:

For the meatballs:

1 onion, 2 garlic cloves

1 bunch dill

1/2 cup long-grain rice

1 1/2 pounds ground beef, 1 egg

salt, freshly ground pepper

sweet paprika to serve

For the sauce:

1 onion

1 2/3 cups meat stock

1 tablespoon butter

1 small organic lemon

salt, freshly ground pepper

2 egg yolks

1 To make the meatballs, peel and very finely chop the onion and the garlic. Wash the dill and shake dry, then finely chop the leaves. Thoroughly wash the rice under cold water and drain.

2 Combine the ground meat with the rice, dill, onion, garlic, egg, salt, and pepper and knead thoroughly. Shape the mixture into small meatballs, about the size of ping pong balls.

3 To make the sauce, peel and finely chop the onion. Put into a wide saucepan together with the stock and the butter and bring to a boil. Reduce the heat to low and place the meatballs into the sauce. Cover with the lid and simmer the meatballs very gently for about 30 minutes.

4 Meanwhile, wash the lemon under hot water and finely grate the zest. Squeeze the juice. Add lemon zest and juice to taste and stir into the sauce. Take one ladle of sauce out of the pot, put into a small bowl, and whisk in the egg yolks. Return to the sauce and heat through briefly. Do not let the sauce boil again or the egg yolks will curdle. Season the sauce to taste with salt and pepper, sprinkle paprika over the meatballs, and serve.

Time you need: 50 minutes
Goes well with: flatbread or rice
Calories per portion: 480

Mixed kebab skewer
Impress your friends!

Serves 4:

For the chicken:

1 pound skinless chicken breasts

1 pinch saffron threads

2 tablespoons lemon juice

4 tablespoons olive oil

salt, freshly ground pepper

For the kofte:

1/2 bunch each cilantro and parsley

1 onion

1 pound ground lamb or beef

1 teaspoon each ground cumin and sweet paprika

1/2 teaspoon Cayenne pepper

salt, freshly ground pepper

about 3 tablespoons oil

For the salad:

3 tomatoes, 1/2 cucumber, 2 red onions

1 bunch mint, 2 tablespoons lemon juice

salt, freshly ground pepper

4 tablespoons olive oil

1 Wash and pat dry the chicken breasts, cut into 3/4-inch cubes. Stir saffron into 1 tablespoon lukewarm water, then stir in the lemon juice and the oil, season with salt and pepper. Stir in chicken; marinate for 4 hours in the fridge.

2 To make the kofte, wash the herbs, shake dry, and finely chop. Peel and finely chop the onion. Add both to the ground meat, season to taste. Add 2 tablespoons cold water and knead everything to a smooth mix. Lightly oil your hands. Take just under 1 tablespoon meat mixture in your hand and shape into a ball, then slightly flatten it. Thread chicken cubes and meatballs alternately onto skewers, brush with remaining oil.

3 To make the salad, wash tomatoes, peel cucumber, cut both into very small dice. Peel and very finely chop the onions. Wash the mint and shake dry , then finely chop it. Combine everything with the lemon juice, salt, pepper, and the oil.

4 Preheat the broiler or a skillet—use a heavy pan with a nonstick coating. Broil or fry the skewers of meat for about 12 minutes, or until they are nicely browned, turning them once. Serve with the salad.

Time you need: 35 minutes
(+ 4 hours marinating)
Goes well with: flatbread and olives
Calories per portion: 595

125

Kibbeh

Sometimes served as an appetizer, but really too filling for that!

Serves 4 as an entrée

or 8 as an appetizer:

For the meat dough:

1 cup fine bulgur wheat

1 pound boneless lamb

1 large onion

1 tablespoon ground cumin

2 teaspoons Cayenne pepper, salt

3 cups oil for deep-frying

For the filling:

1 onion

2 tablespoons olive oil

1/2 pound finely ground lamb

1 tablespoon sumac

1 teaspoon cinnamon

salt

1/2 cup pine nuts

1 To make the meat mix, put the bulgur wheat into a bowl, cover completely with water, leave to swell for about 15 minutes. Cut off the larger pieces of fat and the sinews from the meat, then cut the meat into cubes. Peel and roughly chop the onion. Put the meat and the onion into a food processor to grind (alternatively use a meat grinder set to a fine grind).

2 Drain the bulgur wheat. Combine with the meat, cumin, Cayenne pepper, and salt, and knead well. Place in the fridge for 1 hour for the flavors to mingle.

3 To make the filling, peel and very finely chop the onion. Fry in the oil until transparent. Add the ground meat and fry over a medium heat until it separates into crumbs. Season with sumac, cinnamon, and salt. Stir in the pine nuts.

4 Divide the bulgur meat mixture into 20 evenly sized pieces, and flatten each one in your hands. Cover with about 2 teaspoons of the filling, then enclose the filling in the meat mix. Shape into longish pieces with pointed ends.

5 Heat the oil for deep-frying. Deep-fry the meatballs for about 4 minutes. Lift out with a slotted spoon and drain well on paper towels.

Time you need: 1 1/4 hours
(+ 1 hour resting)

Goes well with: flatbread and cucumber yogurt (without raisins, page 43)
Calories per portion: 420

Speedy version:

Instead of preparing a separate meat mix and a filling, combine everything, shape into balls, and deep-fry.

Variation:

Turkish bulgur rolls

To make the meat mix, soak the bulgur wheat with 1 teaspoon ground cilantro in water. To make the filling, peel and dice 2 onions, then sauté in 2 tablespoons butter. Finely grate 1/3 cup walnuts. Combine with the onions, ground lamb, 1 bunch chopped parsely and 1 teaspoon each cinnamon, ground allspice, ground cumin, and sweet paprika. Knead together and seaon with salt and pepper. Finely chop the bulgur wheat and the cubed lamb as described, then shape into little balls. Cover with filling and close each ball, then deep-fry as above. After draining on paper towels, serve with a spicy tomato salad (page 49) and a cucumber yogurt (page 43, without raisins).

Ramadan soup

The reward for fasting in the Orient — a great winter warmer for us

Serves 4 as an entrée:

1/2 cup dried fava beans

1/3 cup dried garbanzos

1 pound boneless lamb or beef

1 onion

2 tablespoons oil or ghee

1 large pinch saffron threads

1 teaspoon each ground turmeric and sweet paprika

2 teaspoons ground ginger

1 pound tomatoes

1 bunch each parsley and cilantro

1 cup lentils

1 teaspoon cinnamon

1/4 cup long-grain rice

salt, freshly ground pepper

lemon wedges to serve

1 Put beans and garbanzos into separate bowls and completely cover both with water. Leave to swell over night. The following day, drain in a strainer. Squeeze the fava beans out of their hard skins.

2 Cut off larger pieces of fat and sinews from the meat. Chop the meat into dice of about 3/4 inch. Peel the onion and chop it into small dice.

3 Heat the oil or ghee in a Dutch oven. Add the onion and the meat, stir and fry for about 5 minutes all over.

4 Stir the saffron into 1 1/2 quarts luke-warm water and leave to stand briefly, or until the water turns yellow. Add to the meat. Add the beans and garbanzos, and season with turmeric, paprika, and ginger. Reduce the heat to low, cover with a lid, and simmer the soup for about 1 hour, or until the beans are cooked.

5 Cut the stem ends off the tomatoes. Pour over boiling water and leave to stand for a short while. Drain into a strainer and refresh under cold water. Skin tomatoes, chop the flesh into small dice.

6 Wash the herbs and shake dry. Reserve a few cilantro leaves for the garnish, finely chop the remainder. Add to the soup together with the tomatoes and lentils. Season with cinnamon and simmer everything for a further 30 minutes.

7 Mix in the rice, then simmer the soup for a further 20 minutes or so, or until the beans and the lentils are cooked. Season the soup with salt and pepper to taste. Garnish with the reserved cilantro leaves and serve. Serve the lemon wedges separately in a little bowl.

Time you need: 35 minutes
(+ soaking over night and
about 2 1/2 hours cooking time)
Goes well with: flatbread
Calories per portion: 480

Or try this:

When the soup is finished, season it with a little harissa (page 95) to spice things up. And if you don't care to buy beans, peas, and lentils, just stick to one type. However, if you use only lentils, the soup won't taste quite so good.

Fish

Fish in the desert? But of course.

Fish in the desert? Well, it wasn't a problem for Jesus. After all, while he was feeding the masses with the miraculously multiplying bread loaves, he also managed to distribute a few tons of fish among the starving people—although most likely those were dried fish, which the Bedouins also carried with them on their long treks from the shores through the sandy lands.

In the Orient, fresh fish is only of interest in the areas bordering the sea or a waterway, for example on the North African coast or on the banks of the Nile. Commonly it is fried or grilled whole; only rarely is it cut into chunks and braised—for example for a tajine.

The people here are not hesitant with their spices. Fresh herbs, pickled fruits, as well as nuts and dried fruit, may accompany their fish, often in the form of a chilled dip. Mussels, shrimp, or octopus, however, are not on the menu for Muslims, nor for Jews—for these creatures swim without the protection of scales and thus are considered "unclean." But since there are not only Muslims and Jews in the Orient, we've decided to include some recipes for seafood in this chapter too.

What the Orient drinks
Rose lemonade

If you find lemonade too childish, you should try this magical scented version—it might even have been this drink which Sheharazade and her sister used as a refreshment during the hot days in between the 1001 nights. Let's just assume for a moment that we were those two. At the end of the night and its story we'd walk into the rose garden, the pride and joy of every ruler in the Orient. And we would take only the most flawless petals from the unsprayed pink and white roses. The dew drops would already have evaporated from them while the essential oils would still be in place. Of course these roses are beautifully scented, and it is similarly taken for granted that we would not wish to get rid of this perfume by washing them. And now we'll make our lemonade:

To make 4 large glasses, add 1 cup sugar to 1 cup water and bring to a boil in a saucepan. Cook until the sugar has dissolved. Add 2 large handfuls of scented, untreated rose petals. Cover with a lid, and let the syrup cool completely. Squeeze 5–6 lemons and stir the juice into the rose syrup. Leave to steep in the fridge for 1 hour. Pour through a strainer, divide among the glasses, and top up with club soda, seltzer, or sparkling mineral water. And if you like it even more rosy, drizzle a little rosewater into the drink. If you're more daring, add some pink champagne instead of the soda or water.

Living
according...

...to the Moon

If you look at time from a western viewpoint, then around 110 days have been lost over the last 100 years. This is because the peoples in the Orient calculate their own year according to the moon, which gives 10 to 11 days a year less than our sun year. And so the Oriental New Year as well as Ramadan, the month of fasting, move slowly from summer to winter and back.

Up until the year 622 in our calendar, the Orient more or less kept up with the seasons due to a combination of moon and sun years alongside a collection of leap months—then Islam removed any connections with earlier seasons and holidays with the introduction of a new calendar, and thereby created a new rhythm of life with the symbol of the crescent moon. Our year 622 thus became the year zero for Islam.

The Persians attempted to use a mixture of the Islamic lunar calendar and the traditional sun calendar for a further 400 years, until finally the sun was reintegrated as the standard. From then on, the Muslim New Year ,"nauruz," was celebrated on March 21 in our calendar, and 2007 is the equivalent of the Muslim year 1427. Complicated? All you need is to take a little time—then it becomes interesting...

Of daily routine

Devout djin!

I would now like to introduce myself to your friend, but in order to find the best time to do so I would like to know more about your daily routine. Please tell me about it.

Consider first of all that time is a different kind of thing for us than for you; I will tell you more about that later. I will now tell you about the daily routines of my utterly devout and busy friend. I should have taken his example too—for I was turned into a djin because I did not pray at regular times, and now I have to accompany and serve you for 1001 years!

But now all about my friend: Unlike me, he gets up even before sunrise in order to say the first of his five daily prayers. Each time before praying, he will perform the ritual washing which allows him to free himself from the everyday in the eyes of Allah. The second prayer will follow at noon; then there is one in the afternoon. Two more follow just before and just after sunset.

During these times, the stores will remain closed, work is set aside, even for my friend who has to care for his seven children. At each prayer time, the muezzin will call the faithful from his minaret, just as church bells may chime at every full hour. Except that your 24 chimes are matched by only five prayer calls for us. In between, you will have more than enough time to go and pay our friend a visit.

Pickled lemons

Acting simultaneously as salt and spice in the Moroccan cuisine, pickled lemons add a certain something to marinades and refine tajines with their unique and powerful aroma. They're a must-have, if you want to cook North African food. Even a little bit of zest is sufficient to add flavor. But it's a good idea to pickle at least 10 lemons to have a supply—it's not worth the effort for less.

Take 1–1 1/4 cups sea salt and 15 lemons. These should be completely untreated; organic fruit are best. To make absolutely certain that they are clean, wash and brush them under hot water and place them in water over night. Now deeply cut 10 of the lemons at one end with a cross cut (into quarters) so they still hang together at the other end. Sprinkle sea salt on the insides and squeeze the lemons back together. In a tall, narrow glass jar, first add a layer of sea salt, then place a lemon on top, continue with the next four lemons, always sprinkling salt in between. Finish with a layer of sea salt. Squeeze the 5 remaining lemons and add their juice to the fruits in the jar. Leave to stand for 1 day so the juices are drawn out, add a little more water if needed so that all lemons are fully covered. Firmly close the glass jar and put it in a dark, cool spot. You can "harvest" your first pickled lemon after about 1 month.

What does it mean...

...salam aleikum?

"Peace be with you"—this is the pious greeting you can hear all over the Orient, even if at times it is casually shortened to a plain "salam." We wish well for others and ourselves; each should live in peace and let the other live in peace too. This is a perplexing but understandable greeting in a region where fighting is an all too regular occurrence, but where you would also wish to open your door to strangers. If all this is too loaded with meaning, you can simply say "hi," "hello," or "salut." Or "shalom" when meeting Jewish people.

Spicy fried sardines

Marinated the day before

Serves 4:

24 fleshy sardines (about 2 pounds)

flour for coating

1/2 cup sunflower oil for frying

For the chermoula marinade:

1 large bunch cilantro

4 garlic cloves, salt

1 tablespoon sweet paprika

1 tablespoon ground cumin

1 teaspoon freshly ground pepper

1 teaspoon ras-el-hanout (page 113)

3 tablespoons olive oil

1–2 tablespoons lemon juice

For the tomato sauce:

1 pound tomatoes

1 small bunch parsley

2 teaspoons ground cumin

salt, freshly ground pepper

2–3 tablespoons olive oil

For the onion sauce:

4 onions

3 tablespoons olive oil

salt, freshly ground pepper

1 pinch ras-el-hanout (page 113)

1 Wash the sardines and scrape off the scales. Cut off the heads. Slit sardines open on the belly side, unfold. Lift the thick central bone up in one place, using the stem of a spoon. Carefully lift off the bone. Once all sardines are boned, wash again under cold water, drain, then place in a bowl.

2 To make the chermoula marinade, wash the cilantro and shake dry, cutting off the thick lower stalk ends. Peel the garlic cloves and combine with the cilantro. Season lightly with salt, then finely chop together with a large, heavy kitchen knife. Combine the mixture with the spices, oil, and sufficient lemon juice to make a thick and creamy marinade. Pour over the sardines and combine well—it's easiest if you use your hands. Cover the sardines and put in the fridge to marinate over night.

3 The following day, make the sauces. Wash and halve the tomatoes. Cut the stem ends from the halves, then grate the tomatoes using a vegetable grater. Wash the parsley and shake dry. Very finely chop the leaves. Combine with the tomatoes, together with the spices and the oil. Mix well, check the seasoning, then chill in the fridge.

4 To make the onion sauce, peel and very finely dice the onions. In a saucepan or skillet, heat the olive oil and fry the onions over a low to medium heat for about 25–30 minutes, or until they are softened but still only very slightly browned. Season to taste with salt, pepper, and ras-el-hanout. Transfer to a bowl and leave to cool.

5 Dip the sardines into the flour, skin side down, then knock off any surplus flour. Sandwich 2 sardines with the skin side facing out. Heat the oil in a large skillet. Fry the sardine doubledeckers in the oil for about 3–4 minutes on each side. Drain on paper towels, then serve with the two sauces. In Morocco this dish is served hot or cold.

Time you need: 1 hour
(+ marinating over night)
Goes well with: flatbread
Calories per portion: 570

Red mullet in vine leaves
Impressive and not difficult

Serves 4:

about 16 vine leaves (pickled or fresh if available; both are usually available at Greek or Turkish delis)

8 red mullet (about 5 ounces each, gutted and descaled at the fish store or counter)

salt, freshly ground pepper

5 tablespoons lemon juice

2 garlic cloves

1 bunch parsley

6 tablespoons olive oil

1 Prepare the vine leaves. If they are pickled, gently separate the leaves (they tear easily), place them in a shallow dish, and cover them with cold water. Leave to soak for about 10 minutes so they lose some of the flavor of the brine in which they were pickled. Wash fresh vine leaves, if using.

2 Now prepare the fish. Hopefully, they have already been gutted and descaled. If not, hold one fish at a time under cold running water (this is to stop the scales flying through the kitchen), then scrape off the scales with a knife, drawing from the tail in the direction of the head. If you have a special fish descaler, now's the time to use it.

3 After descaling, wash the fish again and pat dry with paper towels. Rub inside and out with salt and pepper. And drizzle with a little lemon juice. Peel the garlic and cut it into thin slices. Wash a few of the parsley stalks and shake dry, then stuff the fish with the garlic slices and the parsley.

4 Place 2 vine leaves at a time next to each other so that the edges overlap slightly. Brush fresh vine leaves with a little oil. Wrap one fish in each set of two leaves.

5 Preheat the broiler or charcoal grill. Brush the fish packages with oil on the outside and grill in the broiler or on the barbecue for about 5 minutes on each side.

6 Meanwhile, wash the remaining parsley and shake dry. Pull off the leaves and finely chop them. Combine with the remaining lemon juice, salt, and pepper, then beat in the remaining oil with a fork until the mixture emulsifies. Serve with the grilled fish.

Time you need: 30 minutes
Goes well with: flatbread
Calories per portion: 335

Or try this:
Fry the wrapped red mullet in a skillet (best of all using a griddle or ridged skillet) for about 5 minutes on each side. You'll only need a small amout of oil for this.

Oven-baked fish
Spiced and layered—
cooks by itself

Serves 4:

2 bunch cilantro

1 onion

4 garlic cloves

6 tablespoons lemon juice

6 tablespoons olive oil

2 tablespoons sweet paprika

2 tablespoons ground cumin

1 teaspoon each freshly ground pepper and
ras-el-hanout (page 113), salt

2 dorades (or porgy—about 1 pound each,
already gutted and descaled)

2 carrots, 4 waxy potatoes

2 green bell peppers

2 young zucchini, 4 tomatoes

1 organic lemon

1 large pinch saffron threads

1 Wash the cilantro and shake dry, pull
off the leaves and finely chop them. Peel
the onion and garlic, dice them as finely as
possible. Combine the cilantro, onion, and
garlic with the lemon juice, 3 tablespoons

olive oil, paprika, cumin, pepper, and
ras-el-hanout. Sprinkle with salt.

2 Wash the fish and pat dry. Score the flesh
by making several cross cuts on each side.
Rub in some of the cilantro sauce. Peel and
thinly slice the carrots and potatoes. Dip into
the cilantro sauce. Line a large ovenproof
dish with the carrots and potatoes. Place the
fish on top, side by side.

3 Wash and clean the peppers, zucchini,
tomatoes, and lemon. Cut the peppers into
rings, the zucchini and tomatoes into slices
about 1/3 inch thick. Thinly slice the lemon.

4 Preheat the oven to 350 °F (convector
oven to 300 °F without preheating). Spread
the zucchini, peppers, and tomatoes over
the fish, add the lemon slices. Combine the
remaining sauce with the remaining oil and
pour over the dish. Dissolve the saffron in
1/2 cup lukewarm water and wait until the
water turns deep yellow. Then pour into the
ovenproof dish. Bake the fish in the center of
the oven for about an hour. Check regularly
and add water if necessary. Filet the fish and
eat with the vegetables.

Time you need: 35 minutes
(+ 1 hour cooking)
Goes well with: flatbread
Calories per portion: 415

Fish on
olive rice
Very easy

Serves 4:

1 1/4 cups long-grain rice (e.g. basmati)

1 red and 1 green bell pepper, salt

1/2 cup pitted green olives

1 bunch scallions

1/2 stick butter

freshly ground pepper

1 pinch saffron theads

3–4 tablespoons lemon juice

4 fish filets (e.g. red mullet, about
6 ounces each)

1 teaspoon each ground turmeric, sweet
paprika, ground cumin, and ground
cilantro seeds

1/4 teaspoon each freshly grated nutmeg
and cinnamon

1 Pour the rice into a colander, rinse under
cold water, drain. Wash and halve the bell
peppers. Remove the stalk and seeds. Dice
the peppers.

2 Put the rice and 2 cups salted water into a saucepan and bring to a boil. Reduce the heat and put the lid on the saucepan. Cook the rice for about 15 minutes, mixing in the diced peppers halfway through.

3 In the meantime, finely chop the olives. Wash and trim the scallions, and cut into fine slices.

4 Preheat the oven to 400 °F (convector oven to 350 °F). Set aside 1 tablespoon of butter, dice the rest. Combine the butter, the olives, and the onion rings with the rice. Season to taste with salt and pepper and transfer the rice to an ovenproof dish.

5 Mix the saffron with the lemon juice and set aside for a moment. Wash the fish filets and pat dry. Combine the saffron juice with the spices, add salt and pepper. Spoon part of the saffron juice on the fish. Place the fish filets on the rice, sprinkle with the rest of the juice. Dice the remaining butter and put it on the fish. Bake in the center of the oven for about 12–15 minutes, depending on the thickness of the filets. Serve in the dish.

Time you need: 50 minutes
Goes well with: cucumber salad with pomegranate (page 48)
Calories per portion: 555

Fish ragout with limes
Quickly prepared

Serves 4:

2 onions, 4 garlic cloves

1 pound tomatoes, 1 organic lime

2 tablespoons ghee

1 cinnamon stick

1 teaspoon each sweet paprika and ground turmeric

2 teaspoons ground ginger

4 fish steaks (about 6 ounces each, e.g. monkfish, swordfish, tuna, or halibut

salt, freshly ground pepper

2 teaspoons honey

1/2 bunch parsley or mint

1 Peel and finely dice the onions and the garlic. Remove the stem ends from the tomatoes. Immerse the tomatoes in a bowl of boiling water for 30 seconds, then cold water for 1 minute, until cool enough to peel off the skins. Halve the tomatoes and spoon out the insides. Remove the seeds, finely dice the pulp. Wash the lime and cut into slices about 1/3 inch thick.

2 Melt the ghee in a saucepan. Stir in the onions, garlic, and cinnamon stick— cut in half. Cook for about 10 minutes over a moderate heat while stirring frequently. Mix the ground spices, sprinkle them into the pan, and fry briefly with the rest.

3 Add the tomatoes and lime slices. Pour 1/2 cup water into the saucepan and bring to a boil. Simmer uncovered over a gentle heat for about 10 minutes.

4 In the meantime, wash the fish steaks or filets and pat dry. Sprinkle with salt and pepper. Season the tomato sauce with salt, pepper, and honey. Place the fish in the saucepan, cover, and simmer in the sauce over a gentle heat for about 10 minutes.

5 Wash the parsley or mint and shake dry. Pull off the leaves and finely chop them. Sprinkle over the fish. Serve.

Time you need: 30 minutes
Goes well with: Persian crusted rice (page 100), couscous (pages 96/97), or simply flatbread
Calories per portion: 275

Whole stuffed mackerel
Something really special

Serves 4:

4 mackerel (about 10 ounces each, already gutted and descaled)

5 tablespoons lemon juice

salt, freshly ground pepper

1/2 pomegranate

2 tablespoons pine nuts

1 tablespoon raisins

1 teaspoon ground cilantro seeds

1 bunch scallions

2 garlic cloves

1/2 cup shelled walnuts

1/2 bunch cilantro

3 tablespoons olive oil

2 teaspoons sumac

1 Wash the mackerel and pat dry. Sprinkle 2 tablespoons of lemon juice over the insides. Rub inside and out with salt and pepper. Leave to marinate for at least 30 minutes. (You can also chill them in the fridge for a couple of hours.)

2 For the filling, break the pomegranate into small pieces. Remove the seeds and the white membranes with your fingers. Mix the pomegranate seeds with the pine nuts and the raisins, and season with salt, pepper, and ground cilantro.

3 Preheat the oven to 400 °F (convector oven 350 °F without preheating). Fill the mackerel with the pomegranate mix and place them side by side in an overproof dish. Cover with foil (shiny side facing the fish) and place in the center of the oven. Bake the mackerel for about 30 minutes. Remove the foil and bake for a further 10 minutes.

4 Meanwhile, trim and wash the scallions, then thinly slice them. Peel and finely chop the garlic. Break the walnuts into small pieces or chop them. Wash the fresh cilantro and shake dry. Pull off the leaves and very finely chop them.

5 Combine the scallions, garlic, walnuts, and cilantro with the remaining lemon juice and olive oil. Season to taste with salt, pepper, and sumac.

6 Take the fish out of the oven and spoon over the sauce mix. Serve immediately.

Time you need: 1 hour
Goes well with: flatbread or nutty rice with onions (page 101), and carrot salad with oranges (made from raw carrots, page 50)
Calories per portion: 535

Variation:

Baked trout
Preheat the oven to 400 °F (convector oven to 350 °F). Wash and pat dry 4 trout (about 12 ounces each). Rub inside and out with salt and pepper and place side by side on a tray in the oven. Wash 1/2 bunch (each) mint, parsley, cilantro, and dill and shake dry. Pull off the leaves and very finely chop them. Combine the herbs with 4 tablespoons lemon juice, 2 tablespoons olive oil, salt, and ground pepper. Pour the mixture evenly over the trout. Bake in the center of the oven for about 25 minutes.

Basic Tip
With whole fish it is often much more difficult to tell whether they are cooked. Fish experts tend to advise checking by pulling out a fin: If it comes away easily, the fish is done. But we think at that point the fish may already be a touch overdone. We therefore recommend a different method: Insert a knife into the backbone and gently move the flesh slightly apart. If it has turned opaque, the fish is ready and can be served.

Fish with garlic sauce
Deliciously spicy

Serves 4:

1 thin slice stale white bread

8 garlic cloves

1 cup mixed walnuts, pine nuts, and almonds

1 tablespoon yogurt

6 tablespoons olive oil

4 tablespoons lemon juice

salt, freshly ground pepper

4 fish filets (about 6 ounces each, e.g. haddock, trout, or salmon trout)

1 bunch scallions

1/2 cup pitted black olives

2 tablespoons almond slivers

1 tablespoon butter

1 teaspoon sweet paprika

1 For the sauce, cut off the crust from the bread and soak the bread in lukewarm water for about 10 minutes. Preheat the oven to 425 °F (convector oven 400 °F).

2 Peel and crush the garlic. Grind the nuts. Squeeze the water out of the bread and place the bread along with the nuts, the garlic, the yogurt, and the oil in a mixer or blender. Add lemon juice and mix thoroughly. Season to taste with salt and pepper and keep in the fridge until being served.

3 Wash the fish filets and pat dry. Season with salt and pepper and place side by side in an ovenproof dish. Trim and wash the scallions. Finely chop the scallions and the olives. Mix with the almond slivers. Dice the butter and add the paprika. Spread the mixture over the fish.

4 Place the fish in the center of the oven and bake for 10–15 minutes, depending on the thickness of the filets. Serve the hot fish with the cold sauce.

Time you need: 30 minutes
(+ 15 minutes baking)
Goes well with: flatbread or
spicy potatoes (page 80)
Calories per portion: 545

Fish with pomegranate sauce
Quick and easy

Serves 4:

2 pomegranates

1 onion

2 garlic cloves

1 tablespoon lemon juice

2 teaspoons sugar or honey

4 fish filets (about 6 ounces each, e.g. swordfish, tuna, or salmon)

salt, freshly ground pepper

1/2 teaspoon ground cilantro

2 tablespoons olive oil

1 small bunch mint

1 Cut 1 pomegranate in half and squeeze out the juice. Halve the other pomegranate over a saucepan. Break the halves into pieces. Use your fingers to remove the seeds and the white membrane from each piece and let them drop directly into the pan. Set aside a few of the pomegranate seeds. Pour the pomegranate juice into the saucepan.

2 Peel and finely dice the onion and garlic. Combine 5 tablespoons water, the lemon juice, and sugar or honey with the pomegranates and bring gently to a boil, stirring constantly. Reduce the heat and simmer uncovered for about 15 minutes.

3 Meanwhile, wash the fish filets and pat dry. Combine the salt, pepper, and cilantro and season the fish on both sides. Heat the oil in a large skillet and fry the fish filets over a medium heat 3–4 minutes on each side.

4 Wash the mint and shake dry. Pull off the leaves and very finely chop them. Strain the pomegranate sauce. Season to taste with salt and pepper and mix in the mint. Transfer the fish filets to heated plates and spoon over the sauce. Sprinkle with the remaining pomegranate seeds and serve immediately.

Time you need: 30 minutes
Goes well with: Persian crusted rice (page 100), saffron rice with apricots (page 100), or flatbread
Calories per portion: 255

Or try this:
Don't fry the fish, but poach it for a few minutes in a gently simmering liquid (water with herbs and vegetables). However, the fish will turn a slightly odd color.

Fish filets with sesame sauce
Very easy

Serves 4:

1 pound onions

2 tablespoons olive oil

1 teaspoon hot paprika

4 fish filets (about 6 ounces each, e.g. salmon, sole, or halibut)

salt, freshly ground pepper

1/2 cup sesame paste (tahini)

1/2 cup yogurt, or sour cream, or heavy cream

4 tablespoons lemon juice

1 bunch parsley

1 Peel and halve the onions. Cut them into fine strips. Heat the oil in a skillet, add the onions and the paprika. Fry over medium heat for about 10 minutes, or until softened, stirring constantly.

2 Preheat the oven to 350 °F (convector oven 300 °F). Wash the fish and pat dry. Season with salt and pepper.

3 Place fish filets side by side in an oven-proof dish. Combine the sesame paste with the yogurt or cream, and the lemon juice. If the sauce becomes too thick, add a little water. Season to taste with salt and pepper and spread evenly over the fish. Put the onion strips on top. Place the fish in the center of the oven and bake for about 15 minutes, or until it is done.

4 Meanwhile, wash the parsley and shake dry. Pull off the leaves and very finely chop them. Remove the fish from the oven, sprinkle it with the chopped parsley, and serve immediately.

Time you need: 35 minutes
Goes well with: flatbread, nutty rice with onions (page 101) or saffron rice with apricots (page 100), and cucumber salad with pomegranates (page 48)
Calories per portion: 385

Or try this:
Sprinkle a few pomegranate seeds on the fish before serving. Or add dates, cut into thin strips, to the onions.

Fish kebabs with chili oranges

Good in wraps too

Serves 4:

1 small onion, 2 garlic cloves

4 tablespoons lemon juice

6 tablespoons olive oil

salt, freshly ground pepper

1/2 teaspoon ground cumin

1 1/2 pounds swordfish, tuna, or monkfish

16 fresh bay leaves (use dried leaves only if you cannot get hold of fresh ones), 1 red chili

1 piece fresh ginger (about 1/3 inch long)

2 juicy oranges (at least 1 of which with untreated peel: i.e. organic)

2 green cardamom, 2 tablespoons sugar

1 Peel and very finely chop the onion and the garlic or purée in a food processor. Stir in 2 tablespoons lemon juice and 4 tablespoons olive oil. Season with salt, pepper, and cumin.

2 Wash the fish and pat dry. Dice into cubes of at least 2/3 inch. Thread the fish cubes

and bay leaves alternately on skewers. Cover with the onion mixture and set aside to marinate in a cool place for about 1 hour.

3 Meanwhile, wash the chili and slit it open lengthwise. Remove the stalk and slice the halves into thin strips. Peel and very finely chop the ginger. Wash the untreated orange under hot water, very thinly pare off the zest and chop it finely. Peel both oranges, removing the white pith. Holding each orange over a saucepan to catch the juice, cut the segments from the skin and finely dice them.

4 Place the chili, ginger, and diced orange pieces in the saucepan. Gently squeeze the cardamon pods and add the seeds to the pan. Mix in the remaining lemon juice, the remaining oil, and the sugar. Gently simmer the chili oranges uncovered over a medium heat for about 10 minutes, stirring from time to time. Let the mixture cool and season to taste with salt.

5 Heat the broiler or a ridged skillet. Cook the fish kebabs either under the broiler or in the skillet for about 10 minutes, turning once. Serve with the chili oranges.

Time you need: 35 minutes
(+ 1 hour marinating)
Goes well with: fried flatbread (page 61), tomatoes, lettuce leaves, herbs
Calories per portion: 590

Spicy shrimps

Impressively easy

Serves 4:

1 2/3 pounds tomatoes

1 bunch parsley

1/2 bunch mint

2 garlic cloves

2 teaspoons ground cumin

salt

1 teaspoon sugar

1 teaspoon harissa (page 95)

4 tablespoons olive oil

1 1/2 pounds peeled raw shrimp (if unavailable, use cooked or frozen shrimp instead)

1 Remove the stem ends from the tomatoes. Immerse the tomatoes in a bowl of boiling water for 30 seconds, then cold water for 1 minute, until cool enough to skin. Very finely dice the peeled tomatoes.

2 Wash the herbs and shake dry. Pull off the leaves and very finely chop them. Peel and crush the garlic.

3 Pour the oil into a saucepan. Add the tomatoes, herbs, garlic, cumin, salt, sugar, and harissa. Simmer uncovered over a moderate heat for about 10 minutes.

4 Wash the shrimp. If you see a black line running down the back, remove it by making a small cut and pulling out the dark intestine. Wash the shrimp again and add to the tomato sauce. Reduce the heat, cover, and simmer for about 5 minutes. (If you bought cooked shrimps, just heat them briefly in the sauce.) Check and adjust the seasoning, if necessary. Serve.

Time you need: 30 minutes
Goes well with: flatbread
Calories per portion: 240

Grilled squid with date paste
Perfect summer dish

Serves 4:
1 2/3 pounds squid (small ones that can be broiled whole, or chopped squid—but do not use octopus, that's the beast with the suckers on its legs!)
salt, 2 teaspoons cumin
1 teaspoon cilantro seeds
2 tablespoons lemon juice
3 tablespoons olive oil
salt, freshly ground pepper

For the date paste:

1 lime, 2 garlic cloves
2 scallions
1 cup fresh, fleshy dates
1/2 teaspoon ground turmeric
1 teaspoon ground sumac
1 pinch cinnamon
salt, freshly ground pepper

1 Wash the squid. Leave the small ones as they are and cut the bigger ones into 4 x 2-inch pieces. Bring to a boil 1 quart salted water. Add the squid and keep on the boil for about 1 minute. Drain in a colander, rinse under cold water. Drain again.

2 Dry-roast the cumin and cilantro seeds in a skillet to release the full aroma. Very finely crush them in a mortar. Combine the spices with the lemon juice and the olive oil. Add salt and pepper. Stir into the squid, and chill in the fridge for 2 hours.

3 Wash and brush the lime under hot water. Finely grate the zest. Squeeze the lime. Peel and crush the garlic. Trim and wash the scallions and very finely chop them. Remove the pits from the dates.

4 Finely purée the dates with the garlic and 3 tablespoons lime juice. Combine with the lime zest, scallions, turmeric, sumac, and cinnamon. Season to taste with salt and pepper and a little more lime juice, if required.

5 Heat the broiler or charcoal grill. Remove the squid from the marinade and grill for about 10 minutes, turning once or twice. Serve with the date paste.

Time you need: 25 minutes
(+ 2 hours marinating)
Goes well with: flatbread and carrot salad (page 50) or orange salad (page 46)
Calories per portion: 275

Sweets &

Here comes the Oriental patisserie

Cakes

And as is usual in cookbooks the desserts come last, even though, in the Orient, after the full meal fresh fruit is more commonly found. The real reason for this is that people are far too fond of all the sweet foods like honey, cane sugar, and marzipan to wait until the end of a meal to enjoy them.

People here treat themselves to a few dates for breakfast, crispy croissants with heavenly fillings as a snack with tea or coffee, and if need be a platter full of rice pudding with all kinds of spices as a main course. Even couscous can be served in this manner.

Fruit does not necessarily have to be served in its natural state. Sherbet is an invention of the Orient, as are candied and dried fruits. The final proof of sugary know-how from Marrakesh to Tehran is the cake shops. You will find Baklava there, and you will find it here—the sweet finale on page 155.

What the Orient drinks
Boza

"Booooooozzzaaaaa" is the cry of the traders in winter as they pass through the streets of Istanbul in an attempt to make the mouths of the passers-by water with the thought of the slightly fermented, sweet-and-sour drink made from bulgur wheat that is so typical of the colder months in Turkey. There are extremely complicated and well-guarded secret recipes for preparing boza which require the skill of a master brewer. There are, however, also simpler methods:

To make around 1 quart, first mix 2 heaped teaspoons of bulgur with 2 cups of water and leave to soak overnight. Then add 2 more cups of water, and, over low heat, stir to a thick smooth porridge, which should take about 20–30 minutes.

The mixture should then be pressed through a fine strainer (if you are in a hurry, you can purée it, but we have lots of time). Then mix in 2 cups of sugar, cover with a cloth, and place on a radiator or in another place that is heated to around 100 °F.

After 3–4 days, the mixture will start to bubble and that is when it is ready.

Now pour the boza into glasses, top each one with a pinch of cinnamon, and drink with a loud slurp. What is left over should be well sealed and stored in the refrigerator, where it can be kept for one or two days.

Sweet
gold...

...brings riches

If you eat something sweet, you immediately feel a little wealthier, happier, and livelier. This is why sweet foods play such an important role in Oriental cuisine, where opulence is loved, but frequently only meager pickings are available. Yet sweet foods are rarely desserts here (for that we have fresh or dried fruits and cakes as snacks)—they are instead terrific entrées in their own right. Those who have been fortunate enough to taste Turkish halva, or baklava, or Moroccan honey pancakes know what I mean.

The happiness-inducing sweetmeats often still have symbolic value, especially if the contain saffron, as they often do in Persian cuisine. "Scholeh Sard," a rice pudding with almonds and saffron, is specially prepared for funeral ceremonies, while a saffron and semolina cake is eaten by the grieving for the first three days following the death, and distributed among the family, the neighbors, and the needy on the seventh and fourteenth days.

A happier occasion calls for "katschi," a saffron cream that is traditionally served to mothers on the day after they have given birth. Thus the mother regains strength and the new birth is suitably celebrated. If you look for the recipe in this book, you will not find it. It is as complicated as haute cuisine in Iran can be—and that's not Basic!

Taking time

Patient Djin!

It is done, I visited our friend. And it was as you predicted. Yet it was also different. At any rate, in the end we lay in the cool shade of a tree in his garden and had a siesta, the first of my life. Where does this laidback attitude come from?

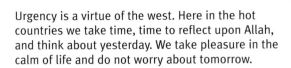

Urgency is a virtue of the west. Here in the hot countries we take time, time to reflect upon Allah, and think about yesterday. We take pleasure in the calm of life and do not worry about tomorrow.

This is why your printed album with seven fields per week—a diary—is for us a book with seven seals. It reminds me of the time of the Pharaohs, when I flew over the countries upon a carpet. Every field was the same size and its calendar of fruit, planting, and harvest was fixed. But what happened to the Pharaohs' gold? In the same manner as they divided up nature, so they divided up the day, into hours and minutes, into meetings and duties, so that in the end nothing was left.

My clock is the sun and it says to me: The day begins when I rise and ends when I lie down. Only once the sun's rays have obliterated the darkness do I take pleasure in a new day. One thing after another. After all, I have all the time in the world—I am a spirit! As is God's will—inshallah!

Home-made Oriental Basics

Fig reçel

This mixture of jam and compote comes from Turkey, and is served not only with light bread for breakfast, but also with tea when guests are present. Reçel can be made from all kinds of jam fruit. Here, to celebrate our Oriental Basics, we will use figs. Green or purple is a matter of taste, just as long as they are good and fresh.

Combine 1 pound of spotless and well-washed figs with 1 pound of superfine sugar, and soak overnight. The next day, boil the juice which has accumulated together with 1/2 cup of water in a saucepan. Add the figs as well as the juice of 1/2 lemon, and simmer the mixture for about 30 minutes, or until the liquid has the consistency of a syrup and the figs are nicely softened. Pour the mixture into jars while hot, seal well, and leave to cool. In a cool and dark place, fig reçel will keep for many months.

What does it mean...
...tse, tse?

It is easier to describe than it is to write—this short and quick flick of the tongue behind the front teeth, where the "ts" is inhaled rather than exhaled and which is almost automatically accompanied by a shake of the head. "Ts, ts" or "tse, tse" is, as an onomatopoeic head shake, an important expression of Oriental body language. It can signify both mild amazement or a gentle rebuke, both of which grow in urgency and importance when accompanied by raised eyebrows, closed eyes, or dramatically rolled eyes. It can also stand for a mildly annoyed or a fatalistic "oops," if something does not go quite according to plan. If a complaint is to be added to this general expression, a melodic "woi, woi" is preferable to a sharp "tse, tse."

Yogurt & lemon cake
Wonderfully moist, wonderfully sweet

Sufficient for 1 cake pan (8 x 8 x 2 inches)
and makes around 20 slices of cake:

2 organic lemons

1/2 stick butter

1 1/3 cups yogurt (Greek or Turkish yogurt
is best)

3 medium eggs

3 tablespoons honey

1 1/3 cups semolina

1 1/2 teaspoons baking powder

1/2 teaspoon cinnamon

1 cup superfine sugar

1 Scrub the lemons under hot water and
thinly grate the zest. Squeeze 1 1/2 lemons.
Preheat the oven to 350 °F (convector oven
to 325 °F without preheating).

2 Melt the butter in a small saucepan, but
do not brown it. Use some of it to grease the
cake pan. Place the yogurt with the eggs,
honey, and the rest of the melted butter in
a bowl and vigorously beat with an electric
whisk. Combine the zest with the semolina,
the baking powder, and the cinnamon. Fold
in the yogurt cream. Transfer the mixture to
the cake pan and bake in the center of the
oven for 35–40 minutes, or until the cake has
risen and is slightly brown on the top.

4 Meanwhile, place the sugar with
1 1/4 cups water and the lemon juice in a
saucepan and bring to the boil over a
moderate heat, stirring until the sugar has
dissolved. Boil the sugary water for about
15 minutes, or until it starts to thicken and
becomes syrupy. Remove from the heat.

5 Remove the cake from the oven. Using a
thin metal skewer, prick the cake all over to
make a large number of holes. Spoon over

the sugar sirup. Let the cake cool. Chill for half a day to infuse. The cake definitely tastes best straight from the fridge.

Time you need: 20 minutes
(+ 40 minutes baking and cooking,
and 1/2 day infusing)
Goes well with: (not typical but divine) whipped cream or ice-cream
Calories per slice: 145

Stuffed dates
Quick to make, quick to disappear

Enough for 12 dates:

12 fresh, fleshy dates (if they are small, you need more)

1/2 organic orange

1/2 cup ground pistachios (unsalted!)

1/2 cup ground almonds (blanched)

1 tablespoon honey

1 tablespoon sugar

1 tablespoon rosewater or orangewater

1 pinch ground cinnamon

12 blanched almonds

1 With a sharp knife, slit the dates open lengthwise and remove the pits.

2 Wash the half orange under warm water and finely grate the zest. Combine the pistachios and almonds with the honey, sugar, rose or orange water, zest, and cinnamon. Knead and divide into 12 pieces.

3 Shape the pieces into strips and stuff them into the dates. Push the almonds into the middle of the dates. You are done!

Time you need: 15 minutes
Calories per piece: 90

Marzipan croissants
Also known as "gazelle" croissants

Makes about 60 croissants:

For the filling:

2 cups whole almonds

3/4 cup superfine sugar

1 small egg

1/4 teaspoon cinnamon

4 tablespoons rosewater

For the pastry:

1/2 stick butter

2 cups all-purpose flour + flour to work

1 pinch salt

3 tablespoons orangewater

For coating and sprinkling:

1 tablespoon melted butter

powdered sugar

1 Place the almonds into boiling water and boil for about 10 minutes. Drain them in a colander, rinse them under cold water, and skin. (You can of course buy almonds which are already skinned, but they are usually quite expensive.) Place the almonds on a dish towel and let them dry for a few hours or, even better, over night.

2 To make the pastry, melt the butter without browning it. Combine the flour with the salt. Add the butter, orangewater, and about 3 tablespoons water. Knead until the dough is very smooth. This may take an exhausting 10 minutes. Wrap in a cloth and leave to rest for 30 minutes.

3 To make the filling, finely chop the peeled almonds in a food processor. Add the sugar and thoroughly mix. Stir in the egg, cinnamon, and rosewater.

4 Thinly roll out the dough on a lightly floured work surface. Cut into strips about 4 inches long and 2 1/2 inches wide. Place 1 teaspoon almond marzipan, formed into a roll, on each strip. The marzipan roll must be smaller than the strip of pastry. Fold the pastry over the marzipan and press firmly together at the edges to seal. (Repeatedly dip your finger in flour.) Shape each one into a little crescent.

5 Line a cookie sheet with baking parchment. Once you have shaped about half of the croissants, preheat the oven to 400 °F (convector oven to 350 °F).

6 Place the croissants on the cookie sheet and bake in the center of the oven for about 15 minutes, or until slightly brown. Brush the hot croissants with butter, and sprinkle with powdered sugar.

Time you need: 1 1/2 hours
(+ 3 x 15 minutes baking time)
Goes well with: strong coffee
Calories per piece: 60

Rhubarb sherbet

Spring is in the air

Serves 6:

1 pound rhubarb

3/4 cup superfine sugar

2 tablespoons rosewater

1 pinch cinnamon

2 drops red food coloring

mint to garnish

1 Wash and trim the rhubarb. Pull off the strings, if necessary. Cut the rhubarb into slices.

2 Place the rhubarb in a saucepan, add the sugar and 2/3 cup water. Bring to a boil, reduce the heat, cover, and simmer for about 10 minutes, or until the rhubarb is soft.

3 Leave the rhubarb to cool, then put it in a food processor together with its juices. Purée, transfer to a bowl, and stir well to combine. If the purée is stringy, pass it through a strainer.

4 Combine the rhubarb purée with the rose water, cinnamon, and food coloring. Place the bowl in the freezer compartment of the refrigerator and leave it to freeze for about 4 hours, until the rhubarb mixture becomes firm. Stir frequently to make sure that the mixture solidifies evenly.

5 Take the rhubarb sherbet out of the freezer 10–20 minutes before serving, and leaving it standing at room temperature. Transfer to dessert bowls and garnish with mint leaves.

Time you need: 30 minutes
(+ 4 hours to freeze)
Goes well with: marzipan croissants
(page 147)
Calories per portion: 90

Variation:

Watermelon sherbet
Use 1 pound watermelon (weight without skin). Remove all seeds with the tip of a knife. Dice the melon and place in a food professor. Add 3 tablespoons light honey and 1/4 cup powdered sugar and purée until smooth. Season to taste with the grated zest of half an organic lemon, 2 tablespoons orangewater, and a pinch of ground cilantro. You can also add some grated chocolate. Transfer to a bowl and freeze for about 4 hours. Stir frequently and leave to stand at room temperature before serving.

Orange & lime granita

Very refreshing after a big meal

Serves 4:

5 oranges (1 organic)

1 organic lime

1/3 cup superfine sugar

1/2 teaspoon cinnamon

2 tablespoons orangewater

To garnish:

mint leaves

ground cinnamon

1 Wash and brush the organic orange and lime under hot water and finely pare off the zest. Squeeze all the oranges and the lime.

2 Pour the orange and lime juices into a saucepan, add the sugar and heat until the sugar dissolves, stirring frequently. Tranfer to a bowl, combine with the cinnamon, the orangewater, and the zest. Leave the mixture to cool.

3 Place the bowl in the freezer compartment of the refrigerator and leave for about 4 hours, or until the juice mixture becomes firm. Stir occasionally, but not as frequently as when you are making sherbet or ice-cream. Granita is not supposed to be as smooth in texture.

4 Crush the ice into fairly large pieces and tranfer to dessert bowls or glasses. Garnish with mint leaves, sprinkle with cinnamon, and serve.

Time you need: 30 minutes
(+ 3–4 hours freezing time)
Goes well with: marzipan croissant
(page 147)
Calories per portion: 100

Basic Tip:

The zest of bitter oranges (Seville oranges) offers a very special aroma. You can find these oranges in winter, especially at vegetable markets or in organic stores. Only grate a very little of the zest and slowly stir it in the juice, together with the zest of ordinary oranges. Regularly taste to avoid using too much of the bitter orange zest, since it would make the granita taste bitter rather than fruity.

Pistachio ice-cream
Always delicious

Enough for 4:

1 cup shelled pistachio nuts (unsalted!)

2 1/2 cups milk

1 organic orange

5 egg yolks

1 cup superfine sugar

1/2 cup yogurt

2 tablespoons orangewater

1 pinch ground cloves

1 Finely chop 2 tablespoons pistachio nuts and set aside. Finely grind the remaining nuts in a food processor. Put into a saucepan, add the milk, and bring to a boil. As soon as the milk boils, remove the saucepan from the heat and set the milk aside to steep for about 30 minutes.

2 Line a strainer with a paper towel and strain the pistachio milk. Drain, twisting the paper towel to collect all the liquid.

3 Wash the orange under hot water and finely grate the zest. Sqeeze the orange. Reheat the pistachio milk.

4 Place the egg yolks in a bowl, add the sugar, and beat vigorously. Slowly add the warm pistachio milk, stirring constantly.

5 Tranfer this cream to a saucepan and heat, stirring constantly. Under no circumstances must the cream be allowed to boil, because the egg yolks would curdle. Keep heating until the cream is thick in texture. Transfer to a bowl and leave the cream to cool a little.

6 Combine the cream with the chopped pistachio nuts, the zest and juice of the orange, the yogurt, orangewater, and cloves. Put the bowl in the freezer compartment of the refrigerator and leave it for about 4 hours, until the mixture becomes firm. Stir frequently to make sure that the pistachios are evenly mixed into the ice-cream, and the ice-cream is very smooth in texture.

Time you need: 50 minutes
(+ 4 hours to freeze)
Goes well with: fresh salad of pineapple, dates, and pomegranate seeds
Calories per portion: 565

Fig yogurt with honey

Perfect breakfast treat

Serves 4:

1 cup dried figs

1/2 organic lemon

1 tablespoon butter

3/4 cup slivered almonds and pine nuts, mixed

4 tablespoons liquid honey

400 g creamy yogurt (Turkish or Greek yogurt is best, possibly made from ewe's milk)

1/4 teaspoon cinnamon

1 Finely dice the figs. Wash the lemon under hot water and finely grate the zest. Squeeze the lemon.

2 Melt the butter in a saucepan, add the almonds and pine nuts, and roast over a medium heat until the aroma fully develops. Add the figs and briefly fry. Thoroughly mix in the zest and juice of the lemon and 2 tablespoons honey. Remove the saucepan from the heat and leave it to cool.

3 Combine the yogurt with the fig mixture and transfer it to shallow dessert bowls. Drizzle over the remaining honey in a zigzag pattern, and dust with the cinnamon.

Time you need: 20 minutes
Calories per portion: 335

Variation:

Fresh figs with honey sauce

Wash 8 fresh figs and remove the stem ends. Quarter the figs. If the skin is too thick, remove it. Place the quarters in dessert bowls or on plates. Break up 1 cup walnuts into smaller pieces. Heat 1 tablespoon butter with 1 tablespoon sugar in a skillet, stirring until the sugar dissolves. Add the walnut pieces and continue to fry until they are shiny and release their scent. Sprinkle over and around the figs. Now put 3 tablespoons honey and 2–3 tablespoons lemon juice in the skillet, stirring constantly. Season to taste with orangewater. Pour the sauce over the figs and serve. This goes well with a little yoghurt or cream cheese—and it's just as delicious on its own.

Almond pudding with syrup oranges

Easy to prepare in advance

Serves 4:

For the almond pudding:

1/2 cup ground blanched almonds

1/2 cup rice flour (available in health food stores)

2 1/3 cups milk

1 egg yolk

few drops bitter almond extract

1/2 cup superfine sugar

For the oranges:

6 oranges (1 organic)

1/3 cup superfine sugar

1 tablespoon orangewater

1 To make the pudding combine the almonds and the rice flour with 2/3 cup milk. Stir in the egg yolk. Pour the remaining milk, the bitter almond extract, and the sugar into a saucepan and heat. As soon as the milk starts to boil, reduce the heat and pull the saucepan off the heat for a short time (set

the saucepan on a wooden board next to the cooker). Whisk the almond rice mixture into the warm milk.

2 Heat the cream for about 5 minutes, or until it starts to thicken without bringing it to the boil, stirring constantly. Transfer the almond cream to dessert bowls and chill for at least 2 hours.

3 To make the syrup oranges wash and brush the organic orange and very thinly pare off the zest. Cut into very thin strips. Squeeze 2 oranges. Peel the remaining oranges, removing the pith. Cut the segments away from the skin, removing the bitter white pith at the same time, and place the segments in a shallow bowl.

4 Put the sugar in a saucepan and dissolve it over a medium heat. Add the zest and juice of the oranges and bring to a boil. At first, the sugar will become solid but then it will again dissolve. Simmer the juice until it reduces and thickens. Leave to cool, stir in the orangewater, and pour over the oranges. Chill for 1–2 hours and serve with the almond pudding.

Time you need: 30 minutes
(+ 2 hours chilling)
Calories per portion: 400

Apricot yogurt cream
Delicious on bread

Serves 4:

1 cup dried apricots (the dark, unsulfurized ones are best)

2 tablespoons superfine sugar

1/2 cup shelled pistachios or pine nuts

1/2 organic lemon

1 cup yogurt

1 teaspoon cinnamon

1 Dice the apricots and put them in a saucepan. Add 1 cup water and leave to soak for 2 hours. Heat and stir in the sugar.

2 Reduce the heat, cover, and simmer for about 15 minutes over a low heat, or until the apricots are soft.

3 Drain the apricots, but make sure you reserve the cooking liquid, part of which we'll be using later.

4 Finely chop the pistachios or pine nuts. Lightly dry-roast them (without oil), if you like a roasted flavor, stirring constantly. Wash the lemon under hot water and finely grate the zest. Squeeze the lemon.

5 Purée the apricots with half the yogurt and the lemon juice in a food processor. If the cream is too thick, spoon in some of the cooking liquid from the apricots, stirring constantly. Stir in the chopped pistachios or pine nuts as well as the zest and cinnamon. Transfer the cream to dessert bowls. Serve the remaining yogurt on the side, or add 1 tablespoon to each portion.

Time you need: 30 minutes
(+ 2 hours marinating)
Goes well with: marzipan croissants
(page 147)
Calories per portion: 325

Sweet saffron rice

Served as a dessert at Turkish wedding banquets

Serves 4:

3/4 cup short-grain rice

1 quince (can be replaced with

1 apple or 1 pear)

1/2 cup superfine sugar

1 large pinch saffron threads

1 tablespoon lemon juice

1 tablespoon each shelled pistachios,

slivered almonds, and pine nuts

1/4 cup raisins

1 pomegranate

1 Pour the rice in a colander and wash under cold water. Drain and place in a saucepan. Add 2 cups water.

2 Wipe the quince with a cloth, cut it into quarters, and remove the core (the easiest way is to cut from both sides and break the core from the quince). Peel and finely dice the quince.

3 Add the quince and the sugar to the rice and bring to a boil. Reduce the heat to very low, cover, and gently simmer the rice for about 15 minutes.

4 Dissolve the saffron in 4 tablespoons warm water and leave to steep until the water turns deep yellow. Add the saffron water to the rice, stir, and simmer for a further 10 minutes, until the rice is cooked.

5 Combine the rice with the lemon juice, tranfer to dessert bowls, and leave to cool. Finely chop the pistachios and dry-roast them with the almonds and pine nuts in a skillet (without oil) for 1–2 minutes, until golden, stirring constantly. Put the raisins in a colander and wash under warm water, then drain.

6 Halve the pomegranate und break the halves into pieces. Pull the red seeds, using your fingers. Remove the white skins, because they taste bitter.

7 Sprinkle the pistachios, almonds, pine nuts, raisins, and pomegranate seeds over the rice and serve.

Time you need: 50 minutes
Calories per portion: 350

Variations:

Sweet couscous

Place 1/2 cup raisins or diced dried apricots in a colander and wash under lukewarm water. Bring to a boil 1 cup water with 2 tablespoons sugar and a pinch of salt. Remove from the heat, stir in 1 cup instant couscous, cover, and leave to stand for 5 minutes. Add the raisins or apricots, 3 tablespoons orangewater, the grated zest of 1/2 organic orange, and 2 teaspoons cinnamon, and stir well to combine. Transfer to little molds, previously rinsed under cold water, press down, and turn onto plates. Sweeten 1 cup buttermilk with sugar and cinnamon and pour around the rice. Garnish with mint leaves.

Couscous with fruit

Cook the couscous as described above. Stir in the juice of 1 orange and 1 tablespoon honey. Leave the couscous to cool. Remove the zest and pith from 1 orange. Cut the fruit segments from the zest and dice. Take the pits out of 10 fresh, fleshy dates and cut the dates in strips. Dice 10 prunes. Halve 1 pomegranate, break it open, and remove the seeds. Combine the fruit with the couscous. Garnish with toasted almond slivers and sprinkle with cinnamon.

Tip:

Replace the rice or couscous with bulgur wheat. Cook like instant couscous – just add a little more water and allow 10 minutes for the bulgur wheat to be ready.

Briouats with fruit

A dream—lovely and sweet

Makes about 22 briouats:

1/2 cup dried apricots

3/4 cup fresh, fleshy dates

3 oranges (1 organic)

1/2 organic lemon

1 cup whole blanched almonds

3/4 cup raisins

1/2 teaspoon ground cinnamon

1/2 stick butter

2–3 sheets yufka or filo pastry

1/3 cup honey

1 Dice the apricots and soak in lukewarm water for about 15 minutes. Remove the pits from the dates.

2 Wash the organic orange and the lemon under hot water and very finely grate the zest. Squeeze all oranges and the half lemon (you should obtain 2/3 cup liquid). Dry-roast the almonds in a skillet over a medium heat, until they turn golden in color.

3 Drain the apricots. Purée the apricots with the dates, the almonds, and 1/2 cup of the orange juice mixture in a food processor. Stir in the raisins and season to taste with cinnamon and zest. Melt the butter, but do not brown it.

4 Carefully separate the pastry sheets and cut them into strips about 4 inches wide and 10 inches long. Brush them with a little melted butter.

5 And now try to imagine how to fold the strips into triangles. Start on the left: Spread 1 tablespoon filling onto the bottom right of the first third of the strip. Fold the upper left corner over the filling on the bottom right and you have your first triangle. You now fold this completely to the right, then upward and then again to the right. The bit of pastry that remains should simply be folded over the triangle. (You will find illustrated step-by-step folding instructions on page 65. Just check it out and have a go.)

6 Preheat the oven to 400 °F (convector oven to 350 °F without preheating). Line a cookie sheet with baking parchment. Place the triangles on the tray and brush them with the remaining butter. Bake in the center of the oven for 12–15 minutes, or until a delicious golden brown.

7 Pour the remaining juice mixture and the honey into a saucepan and bring to a boil. Boil for a few minutes. Dip the briouats one by one into the syrup, remove them with a slotted spoon, and leave to cool.

Time you need: 1 hour
Goes well with: fresh fruit such as oranges, or apricots, or peaches, but also strawberries and cherries
Calories per portion:130

Or try this:

Do not fold the pastry into triangles, but cut it into smaller pieces and shape it into rolls. Deep-fry the rolls in very hot oil for about 3–4 minutes, or until golden brown. Drain and serve lukewarm, without the syrup.

Variations:

Date filling
Remove the pits from 1 2/3 cups fresh, fleshy dates. Dice the dates and purée them with 2 tablespoons orangewater. Combine with the grated zest of 1 washed organic orange, 1/2–1 teaspoon cinnamon, 1 pinch of ground chili pepper, and 1 egg white. Roll into the pastry strips, deep-fry, and dip in the syrup.

Almond filling

Place 2 cups almonds in a saucepan, add water and bring to a boil. Boil for about 5 minutes, drain, and rinse under cold water. Skin the almonds and chop them. Put in a food processor, add 1/3 cup runny honey and 3 tablespoons orangewater and purée. Mix in the grated zest of 1/2 organic lemon and 1 large egg. Season to taste with ground cinnamon. Place the filling on the pastry strips and shape into rolls. Deep-fry, drain, and dip in the syrup.

Baklava
The perfect recipe to enchant your friends

Serves 8–10:

1 2/3 cups shelled walnuts

1 1/2 cups blanched almonds

2 egg whites

1/3 cup superfine sugar

1 teaspoon cinnamon

2 tablespoons orangewater

1 stick butter

10 ounces yufka or filo pastry

1/2 cup shelled pistachios

For soaking:

3 oranges

1 lemon

2/3 cup honey

1 Very finely chop the walnuts and almonds, or grate them with a nut grinder. Beat the egg whites until stiff, while gradually beating in the sugar and cinnamon. Fold in the chopped nuts with the orangewater.

2 Preheat the oven to 350 °F (convector oven to 325 °F without preheating). Melt the butter without browning it. Choose a large rectangular ovenproof dish. Carefully separate the pastry sheets and cut them to the size of the dish.

3 Grease the ovenproof dish with a little butter. Place one pastry sheet in the dish, brush with butter, and add another sheet. Butter again, then thinly spread with the nut mixture. Continue to alternate 2 buttered pastry sheets and the nut mixture, ending with a final layer of pastry. Always brush the pastry with butter. Using a sharp knife, mark 2 x 2-inch squares. Bake in the center of the oven for about 40 minutes, or until the cake is golden brown in color.

4 Finely chop the pistachios. Squeeze the oranges and lemon, pour the juice in a saucepan, and heat it with the honey. Leave the honey sirup to cool slightly, then pour it over the cake. Sprinkle the cake with the pistachios, leave it to cool and infuse, if possible over night.

Time you need: 30 minutes
(+ 40 minutes baking
and 1 night steeping)
Calories per portion (10 pieces): 600

Or try this:

If you are not particularly fond of honey or forgot to buy some, you could make your own syrup. Add water to the citrus juice, topping it up to 1 2/3 cups, mix in 1 cup sugar, and bring to a boil. Simmer the juice until you have a thick syrup. Instead of the honey mixture, pour the syrup over the baked cake.

You can also use puff pastry instead of yufka or filo pastry. Thaw frozen pastry sheets and roll out as thinly as possible on a lightly floured surface. Layer the pastry and the nut mixture alternately into an ovenproof dish, but only use a single layer of puff pastry each time. Bake as above.

Index